Value-Based COST MANAGEMENT *for* HEALTHCARE

Linking Costs to Quality and Delivery

KICAB CASTAÑEDA-MÉNDEZ

QUALITY RESOURCES®
A Division of The Kraus Organization Limited
New York, New York

Most Quality Resources books are available at quantity discounts when purchased in bulk. For more information contact:

Special Sales Department
Quality Resources
A Division of The Kraus Organization Limited
902 Broadway
New York, New York 10010
800-247-8519

Printed in the United States of America

00 99 98 97 96 10 9 8 7 6 5 4 3 2 1

Quality Resources
A Division of The Kraus Organization Limited
902 Broadway
New York, New York 10010
212-979-8600
800-247-8519

∞

The paper used in this publication meets the minimum requirements of American National Standard for Information Sciences—Permanence of Paper for Printed Library Materials, ANSI Z39.48-1984.

ISBN 0-527-76304-7

Library of Congress Cataloging-in-Publication Data

Castañeda-Méndez, Kicab.
Value-based cost management for healthcare : linking costs to quality and delivery / Kicab Castañeda-Méndez.
p. cm.
Includes index.
ISBN 0-527-76304-7
1. Medical care—Quality control. 2. Health services administration. 3. Medical care—Cost control. 4. Medical care—Cost effectiveness. I. Title.
RA399.A1C38 1996
362.1'068—dc20 95-40729
CIP

Dedication

To Marta, Cindy, and Larry.

Contents

Acknowledgments

W. Edwards Deming often said in his seminars and books: First, learn. Then, find how to use that knowledge by theorizing. Fortunately, I did not have to wait until I first heard Deming in 1982 to hear this invaluable advice. My father, a professor of philosophy, also said the same thing—perhaps among the first words he ever said to me.

Value-Based Cost Management is the result of more than four decades of learning. Unsurprisingly, others developed most of the basic concepts into a practical framework.

Learning comes in many forms; experiences, readings, education, thinking. Consequently, many people have contributed. They asked questions; explained what they did; revealed weaknesses in earlier versions of my work; told me directly or indirectly about their successes and failures, which helped me formulate connections among ideas; discussed the ideas with me; and sometimes, they just **listened** to me. Five people who helped in this manner and deserve mention are: my wife Marta Chase; my long time friends David and JoAnn Keosaian; my colleague Dan Follas; and Elia Mears, who provided valuable information for the nutrition examples.

Others made this book a reality. In particular, Larry Bernstein, M.D. of the Bridgeport Hospital, Bridgeport, CT who has been and continues to be an indefatigable source of encouragement, promotion, information, and ideas. Cindy Tokumitsu envisioned a book when others were merely responding to article-length manuscripts and short presentations on earlier pieces of this book. Cindy also contributed through her patience and editorial critiques as I struggled to integrate the many ideas. Randy Pettit helped in reviewing and preparing the typesetting. Valerie Lentz designed the text. Victoria Carlquist and Jackie Valentino of the Ridgefield Library, Ridgefield, CT were especially instrumental in the success of my research efforts.

Introduction

The changes in healthcare over the past decade have been nothing short of astonishing. While the federal government has been spending countless hours and resources debating what to do, the healthcare industry has taken action, initiating several changes that bode well for it and the nation. Five years ago, there was a dearth of healthcare information useful for comparisons, for decision making, or for making measurable progress. Today, numerous organizations have been created to collate such information, and significant changes in a variety of places have taken place because of that information.

Unlike most other industries, healthcare has taken to the quality movement in droves. According to the 1994 annual *ASQC/Gallup Survey Report,* 94 percent of hospitals claim to have a formal quality program in place. Most claim to be total quality organizations. While some hospitals have been swallowed by mergers and consolidations and others no longer exist, the net profit figures for hospitals have increased over the past two years. Some may attribute these positive income changes to quality improvement. Others may attribute it to cutbacks that threaten the quality of healthcare so proudly proclaimed by employees and citizens.

The need for healthcare organizations, their employees, their patients, and this nation to benefit from quality is so great, that it has triggered activities on several fronts:

- Several states not only have a separate quality award category for healthcare organizations, but they also have separate criteria.
- The nation's leading quality award, the Malcolm Baldrige National Quality Award, introduced specific criteria for healthcare organizations in 1995.
- The leading hospital accreditation organization, the Joint Commission for Accreditation of Healthcare Orga-

nizations (JCAHO), has steadily converged on the Baldrige award's criteria as the basis for its accreditation guidelines.

- The leading managed care accreditation organization, the National Committee for Quality Assurance (NCQA), examines the organization's quality improvement program.
- Other healthcare associations have developed awards to recognize quality in healthcare.

While healthcare organizations are reluctant to accept what they call the industry quality model, the change in HMOs from mostly not-for-profit to mostly for-profit makes it almost impossible for these organizations to ignore many lessons already learned by other industries. In fact, only the foolish will choose not to seek knowledge from outside healthcare. Healthcare organizations are no different than other organizations in one fundamental way: they must have revenues that equal or exceed their expenses. The most important lesson is that a total focus on quality is the best way to achieve this in the long run. The critical concern for all organizations is how to profit from quality. The 1995 Baldrige award criteria reflect this concern by putting a greater emphasis on results than previously given.

Starting 30 years ago, and with further refinements during the 1980s, Avedis Donabedian, M.D., of the University of Michigan Medical Center, the father of quality assurance in healthcare, proposed a healthcare framework for assessing quality based on the separation of structures, processes, and outcomes (SPO model). This framework depends on establishing relationships between structures and processes on the one hand, and processes and outcomes on the other. Unfortunately, the sciences (i.e., organizational, behavioral, and healthcare) needed to establish these relationships have not all contributed to the degree necessary. In addition, the model appears incomplete: it does not close the loop by identifying the necessary relationship between outcome and structure and it does not include the science of finance and accounting for establishing the relationships between structures, processes, outcomes, and *costs*.

This book presents a solution to the incompleteness of the SPO model. In addition, it offers a three-dimensional framework connecting quality, delivery, and costs through a value-based cost management system. Third, it resolves the time-quality-cost dilemma that healthcare businesses face—that is, that there must always be trade-offs between these three critical business factors. However, by identifying time as cycle time and quality as freedom of deficiencies, cycle time management actually provides the basis for quality improvement and cost reduction through reduction in time.

The first dimension of this framework comes from a fundamental concept of TQM: organizations can increase their value by creating a work environment that promotes and rewards high-performance and high-satisfaction work teams to produce and deliver high-quality and highly satisfying products and services. For healthcare organizations, this means they can profit from improved patient satisfaction and outcomes through increased employee satisfaction and involvement. To accomplish this, they must identify and track those measures of activities that are customer (i.e., patient) value-added, employee value-added, and business value-added.

The second dimension consists of integrating three ways of analyzing expenses and revenues. These three analyses are done sequentially on items taken directly from the general ledger to:

- More accurately estimate costs to show profitability of services and product lines.
- Identify activities that do not add value to customers, employees, or the business.
- Classify costs to reveal where they can be reduced by improving quality and delivery.

The first analysis, activity-based costing (ABC), focuses on the *management of activities*. By identifying where traditional standard costs are too inaccurate, ABC can be used cost-effectively to obtain more accurate information by individual patient because it assigns costs by reversing the demand flow for resources. Applying ABC to services and product lines helps identify where profits need to be boosted by reducing product and service costs.

The second analysis, value-added (VA) analysis, focuses on the *management of time*. By revealing where there are delays, lead times, and queues, VA analysis can be used on those services and product lines identified by ABC to immediately reduce cycle times and increase productivity—that is, the rate at which value is added.

The third analysis, cost of quality (COQ), focuses on the *management of quality* in terms of costs. After removing non-value-added activities, the remaining activities are classified not according to standard expense classification but according to quality-related expense categories. Rather than saying one hour of a resource was used, COQ says that an hour of a resource was used to prevent nonconformance, produce, evaluate productivity, or correct nonconformance. Any activity used to correct nonconformance (the cost of poor quality) can be reduced by improving quality.

The third dimension of this framework defines the systems needed to support a total quality management effort: leadership, strategic quality planning, human resources, core business, support services, supplier quality, customer satisfaction, and information and analysis. The value-based cost management system can be applied to the organization's efforts to develop and deploy these systems to validate the value of its quality efforts.

This book is divided into nine chapters. The first chapter contains a story to illustrate the most pressing issues in healthcare today—and tomorrow. These issues are represented as a set of nine questions that senior management must be able to answer. These issues are highly relevant to all management levels, indeed to anyone engaged in quality implementation. The senior management perspective is used to provide an encompassing picture and to demonstrate the importance of involvement at that level. This book is about the current tools and methods that are available to answer these questions. The relationship between these tools and methods and the way an organization is structured and operates is described in chapter 2.

In chapter 3, the fundamental concept of quality and continuous improvement, the process, is defined. Virtually everything we do is an instance of a process. Processes do not perform as we expect because of variation in the conditions in which they operate and in what feeds the processes. Process variation affects costs, quality, and delivery of healthcare services and products. The ultimate goal is to eliminate process variation.

The next three chapters describe ABC (chapter 4), VA analysis (chapter 5), and COQ (chapter 6). Reducing process variation and improving process quality are accomplished by practicing continuous improvement. In chapter 7, the continuous improvement cycle system (CICS) is described. The CICS identifies the five major skills required to continuously improve: the ability to analyze quality and delivery in terms of costs, the ability to understand process variation, the ability to gain an in-depth understanding of processes, the ability to solve problems, and the ability to manage cycle time.

Chapter 8 shows how these methods are integrated into the CICS through value-based cost management. By using the procedures described in this chapter on how to collect, interpret, and understand data, the reader will be able to reduce costs by improving quality and delivery through faster cycle time. The sequence for using all the tools to develop the appropriate measures is also illustrated in chapter 8.

The last chapter, chapter 9, shows how these methods can be applied to an organization's quality efforts. In particular, they are applicable to the organizational systems (combinations of processes) that are defined by the Malcolm Baldrige

National Quality Award's categories and that support the JCAHO and NCQA guidelines on quality improvement. Using these methods to evaluate one's quality efforts can result in ever-improving quality throughout the healthcare organization, extending to its customers and suppliers.

1 Linking Costs to Quality and Delivery in Healthcare

You are a senior executive in a healthcare organization reading the front page of the April 26, 1994 edition of *The Wall Street Journal:*

> "Just last month, Digital Equipment Corp.'s chief executive officer, Robert B. Palmer, had reason to believe the loss-plagued computer maker was turning around: Reports from the sales force indicated revenue was holding up and new products were taking off."

You go along with the reasoning, thinking that certainly the CEO would have received the information necessary to reach this conclusion. You also believe that if revenues are steady and new products are selling, things should be picking up. You read on:

> "But Mr. Palmer was jolted by a rude surprise. While product sales weren't bad in the company's fiscal third quarter, service revenue was off sharply, sales costs were rising, and rampant discounting was swallowing any possible profit. The resulting $183 million loss led . . ."

"$183 million loss!" you whistle to yourself. "That's our budget for an entire year." Several questions quickly flash across your mind:

- Why didn't he look at the other indicators?
- Why didn't he have an inkling during the third quarter, instead of finding out in the fourth quarter? I'm glad this couldn't happen to us . . . could it?

Later in the year, you read about the University of Michigan Medical Center's success with its total quality management (TQM) efforts.[1] They claim to have invested $2.5 million in quality efforts and gotten a return of more than $17 million in savings. Your organization has been involved in quality for four years now and you know that this is just the kind of success story many healthcare organizations have reported. You remember attending a conference sponsored by the Institute for Healthcare Improvement, where the Medical Center Hospital of Vermont presented the results of a cardiac surgery team consisting of surgeons, anesthesiologists, nurses, respiratory therapists, and pharmacists that, by focusing on the types of drugs used for heart surgery patients, was able to reduce length of stay by 35 percent and intubation hours by 26 percent, while generating savings for the hospital. You think about Digital and how if only they had used a TQM approach.

A few weeks later, you're talking with the laboratory administrator in your hospital. She is telling you about one of the breakout sessions at the annual Clinical Laboratory Management Association she attended. A pathologist and laboratory director from Shadyside Hospital in Pittsburg, PA, had applied quality improvement tools to address the financial aspect of their acute myocardial infarction process. They reported that a routine audit revealed that Shadyside had lost more than $1 million on the last 151 acute myocardial infarction patients.[2]

---

1. Gaucher, E. and Coffey, R. *Total Quality in Health Care: From Theory to Practice.* San Francisco: Jossey-Bass Publishers, 1993.
2. Smith, William I. and Mack, David. "Utilization Management," Clinical Laboratory Management Association Annual Conference August 27-31, 1994, Orlando, FL.

You're jolted by a rude surprise: $1 million loss! You immediately think of Digital, and the same questions run through your mind. Now you also recall the University of Michigan Medical Center's and the Medical Center Hospital of Vermont's success stories and begin to see a common theme. You say to yourself, "If the University of Michigan Medical Center saved $17 million, that means they had $17 million in losses. In fact, every healthcare success story that says the organization saved money was only possible because they lost that money in previous years. Each year's budget was based on the previous use of resources. If that use was ineffective or wasteful, the next year's budget institutionalized these losses. Why didn't these organizations know that they had such losses to be saved? I wonder what our losses are? Will TQM be enough?"

You recall the profit implications of marketing strategies (PIMS) study of nonhealthcare organizations.[3] It impressed you because it showed that manufacturers and service organizations that produced quality products and services had a significant market advantage. The market-perceived value of the products and services produced a competitive advantage by allowing several approaches to increased profits: the organization could sell the products and services at a premium; it could sell at competitive prices and thereby gain market share and increase revenues through volume; or it could sell at a discount, reducing the competition, and at that point prices could be raised.

"It certainly appears that having a quality culture can compensate for some of these losses by having some quality services yielding higher profit margins," you say to yourself. "But how can I reduce or eliminate losses? How do I know that the cost of these continuous improvement efforts is not greater than the savings? How do I know that any significant savings we find are due to our quality efforts and that these

3. Buzzell, Robert D. and Gale, Bradley T. *The PIMS Principles: Linking Strategy to Performance.* New York: The Free Press, 1987.

efforts also address our critical success factors? Couldn't we be in the same situation as these other organizations? Perhaps some of the PIMS findings are applicable to healthcare now because we are all competing for managed care contracts on price."

Since the number of people in HMOs has increased 40 percent and now more HMOs are for-profit than not-for-profit, running a healthcare organization as a business never made more sense. Even not-for-profit organizations are seeing an increased need for business savvy as they too are suffering from reduced revenues from operations. In addition, the threat of losing market share immediately to managed care contracts hovers over all healthcare organizations.

You recall a recent JCAHO study showed that hospitals complying with more of the JCAHO guidelines tended to do better financially.[4] Perhaps, you think, that all this has to do with the premise behind TQM: provide greater customer ("i.e., patient") satisfaction at reduced operating costs through the efforts of more job-satisfied employees. But you still wonder, "Are we getting the right information and in a timely manner? After all, the message from Digital, the University of Michigan, and Shadyside is: 'If we aren't measuring our losses, we can't be aware of them. If we aren't aware of them, we can't prevent them.'"

"So," you say to yourself, "while raising our prices is not a realistic option, managed care does mean that we must know our costs for *every* service. We just haven't known them. Census . . . adjusted census . . . length of stay . . . these are our typical measures. They aren't good enough."

You pull last quarter's profit and loss statement from your files and sketch a bar chart of the primary numbers (see Figure 1.1). "One-third of our revenues," you calculate from the figures, "come from Medicare and Medicaid. These reimbursements are continually being reduced—and they are no longer sacred under a balanced budget. With our profit mar-

4. "Linking Quality and Finances," *Hospitals*, May 20, 1993.

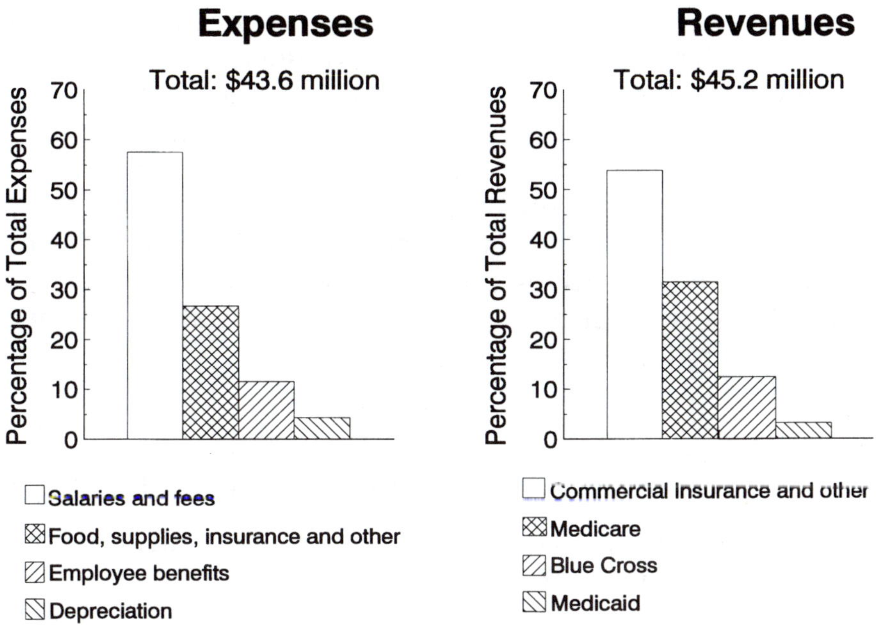

FIGURE 1.1 Sample Bar Charts for Expenses and Revenues

gin of 3.7 percent [lower than average hospital profit margin], we can't afford drastic cuts in these revenues. Salaries, fees, and benefits account for two-thirds of our expenses. Clearly, better management of people's time is critical to controlling costs.

"My task is to use this information along with other kinds of information, to plan the organization's strategic quality initiatives," you say to yourself. "I have to provide direction through strategic issues that require allocation of resources. Our employees then progress toward realization of the strategic goals we set for them. These goals are to achieve specific profit levels by controlling our costs of implementing the strategic plan.

"How does this general ledger information tell me whether we are accomplishing our TQM purpose?" You scan the details of your profit-and-loss statement—and begin to worry. The details only split the total figures into more categories (see Figure 1.2). Total salaries can be divided into salaries by department, which can be divided into salaries by individual employee. You say to yourself, these figures and details don't tell me what contribution employees provided—yet, they are the greatest resource we have no matter how we look at the figures.

"I know that each patient impacts the bottom line. A single patient who receives poor quality and delivery of our healthcare services negatively affects our profitability. What I really need to know is:

- Are my cost estimates accurate?
- What is the net profit and loss for each patient?
- Which activities added value to our patients, employees, and business?
- What is the cost of poor quality and poor delivery of services to each patient?

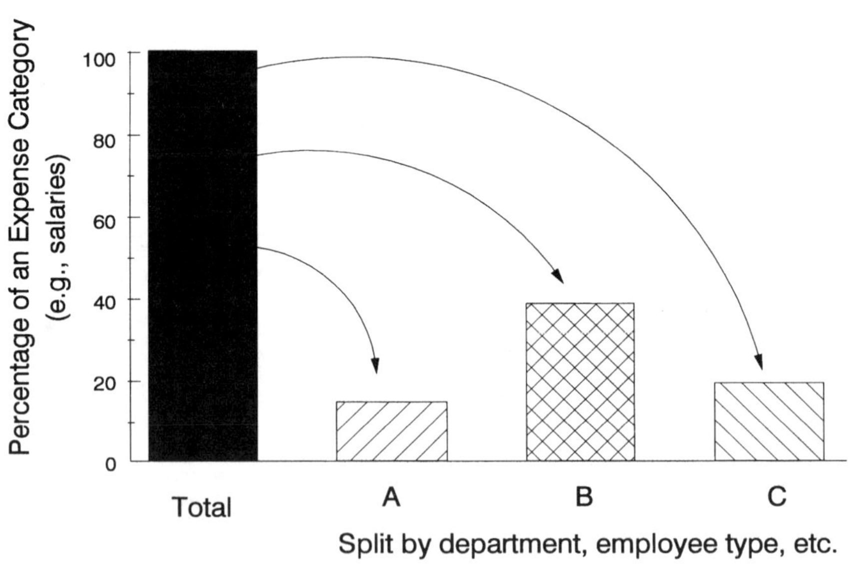

FIGURE 1.2 P & L Statement Details

- What is the cost of poor quality and delivery of services to our employees?
- What skills are needed by each of us to continuously improve?
- How can everyone reduce costs by improving quality and delivery of our products and services?
- How can I financially justify our quality efforts?
- What is my role as a senior manager?"

You realize that the financial information you have cannot answer these questions. It's obvious that expenses and revenues are clearly shown, but quality, delivery, and value to patients and employees are not. In addition, since the profit-and-loss information is maintained by management, employees cannot contribute knowingly to the bottom line even if the information did link quality and delivery to cost.

You—everyone in the organization—need new information and new skills. According to Dennis O'Leary:

> "The one thing missing is that hospitals do not grasp how one moves from the data stage to the improvement stage. In our experience on surveying hospitals across the country, we are struck by the amount of data that hospitals have collected and the fact that data then gathers dust because no one knows what to do with it. Data must be converted into information, and the information has to be used as part of an assessment process."[5]
>
> "The JCAHO Applauds TQM"
> *Health Systems Review,* May/June 1992

5. O'Leary, Dennis. "The JCAHO Applauds TQM," *Health Systems Review,* May/June 1992.

2 The Twenty-First Century Healthcare Organization

NEW MANAGEMENT PHILOSOPHIES

Healthcare organizations have already made changes to cope with new financial pressures, competitive changes in the markets, and threats of reform, but their structures and processes must also change to cope with four organizational revolutions: patient focus, continuous improvement, total participation, and societal networking.[1] These revolutions have forced a change in the management philosophies of the organization's leadership, clinical and operational management marketing, service design, purchasing, patient care units, and accounting (see Table 2.1). The new philosophies hold firmly to the idea that business and organizational success are derived from empowering, educating, and providing resources to employees to provide ever-increasing customer satisfaction. For healthcare organizations, this means identifying patient and community needs; designing high-quality, fast cycle-time, value-adding products and services; collaborating with other stakeholders and suppliers; and providing access to information on quality, costs, and outcomes to all.

Financial data are no longer enough for organizational survival. Nonfinancial data—data on quality and delivery—are also needed, and both must be translated appropriately for continuous improvement. A new cost-accounting system

1. Shiba, Shoji; Graham, Alan; and Walden, David. *The New American TQM: Four Practical Revolutions in Management.* Portland, OR: Productivity Press, 1993.

TABLE 2.1. New Corporate Healthcare Philosophies

Function	New Philosophy
Leadership Management: Clinical and Operational Processes	• Constancy of purpose • Data-based decisions • Learning organization • Short-term action to achieve long-term plans • Collaboration and partnering with suppliers, patients, customers, community, and employees • Continuous improvement
Marketing	• Meet patient and community needs • Identify future patient and community requirements
Service Design	• Design for healthcare promotion and coordination of services • Design for patient perceived-value • Design for low parts per million (ppm) defect rates • Design for reduced cycle-time
Purchasing	• Partnering with vendors • Reduction in number of vendors • Quality certification of vendors • Eliminate inventory
Patient Care Units	• Clinical outcome focus • Patient satisfaction focus • Reduce variation • On-target products and services • Fast cycle-time • Increase access • Process control • Multifunctional value-adding teams
Accounting	• Information for more accurate cost estimates • Information for reducing costs by improving quality • Information for eliminating non-value-added costs • Information for continuous improvement of structurees, processes, and outcomes

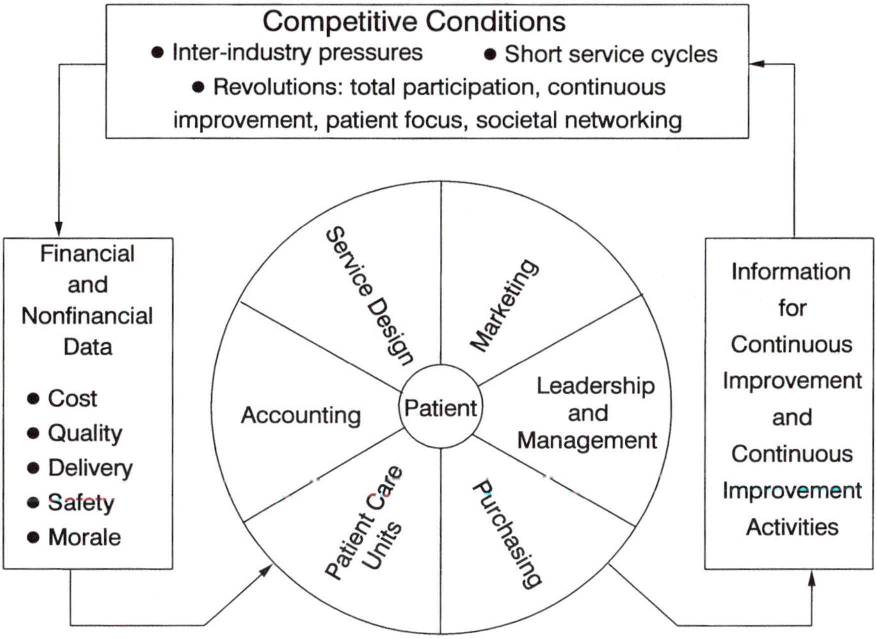

FIGURE 2.1 The New Cost-Accounting Philosophy

is needed for these new philosophies.[2] The new cost-accounting philosophy identifies the patient as the primary customer by including quality and value, supports the other philosophies, promotes an integration of systems, and provides information vital for continuous improvement (Figure 2.1). Management's philosophy is now on becoming profitable *through* patient and employee satisfaction.

THE VALUE-BASED COST MANAGEMENT SYSTEM

An analysis of why organizations fail or abandon their quality efforts suggests that there are four barriers to implementing TQM:

2. Turney, Peter B.B. and Anderson, Bruce, "Accounting for Continuous Improvement," *Sloan Management Review*, Winter 1989, pp. 37–48.

1. Lack of strategic planning.
2. Lack of metrics.
3. Outdated business cultures.
4. Confusion over incremental and reengineering approaches.[3]

In healthcare, other possibilities have been noted. For example, healthcare organizations:

- Often have difficulty in accepting the concept of the patient as a customer.
- Implement TQM from an abstract rather than personal perspective.
- Remain project-oriented rather than seek a cultural transformation.
- Use charts and measurements too early in the roll-out.[4]

A case can be made that these healthcare barriers are symptoms of the four broader barriers, for example, without a strategic plan, the organizational implementation is likely to be project-based; with outdated cultures, turf wars hinder patient-focused team-building; and so on.

Removal of these barriers requires a cost management system that addresses five areas (see Figure 2.2):

1. Patient-focused strategic quality plan.
2. Definition of patient needs and satisfaction.
3. New expense categories and their management systems.

3. Fuchs, E., "Total Quality Management from the Future: Practices and Paradigms," *Quality Management Journal*, October 1993, pp. 26–34.

4. *Modern Healthcare*, January 4, 1993.

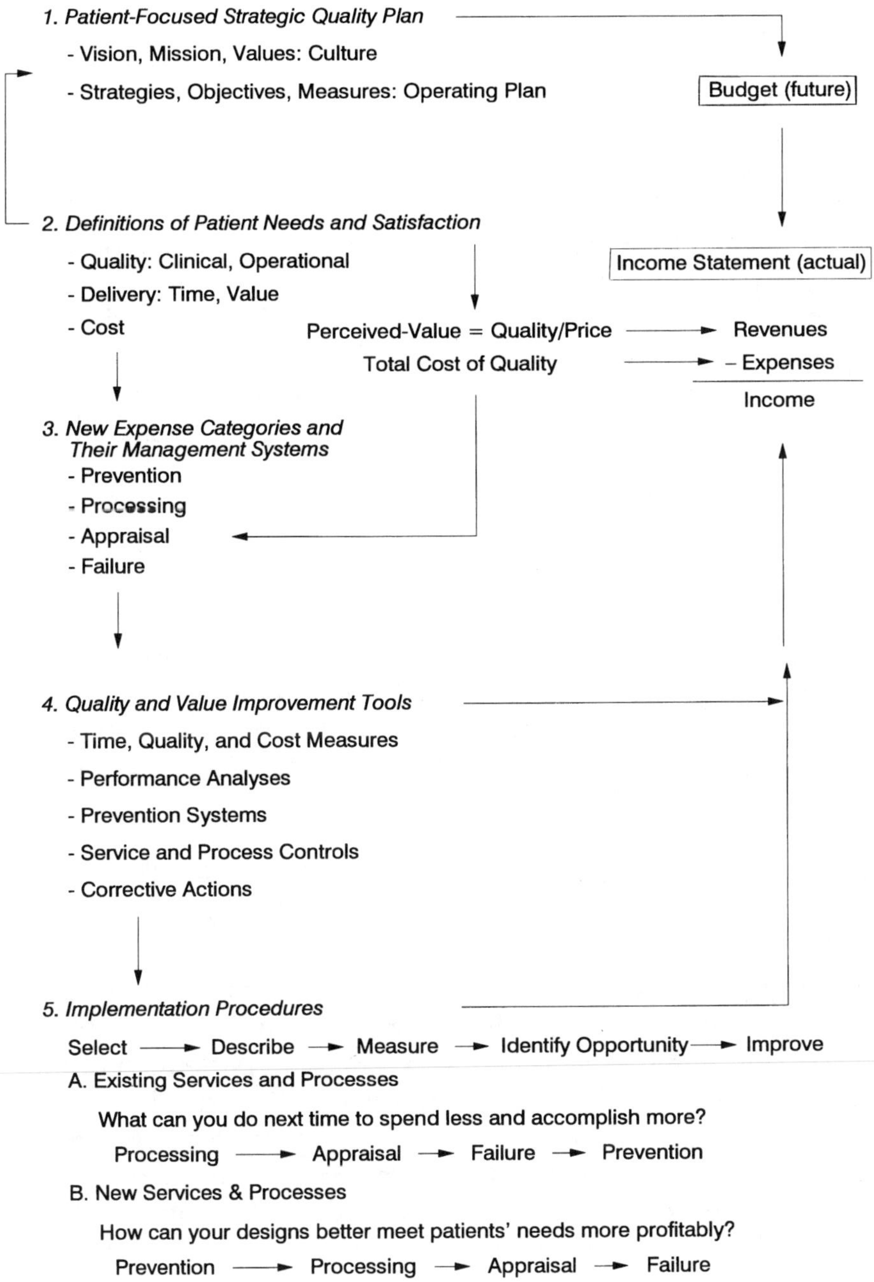

FIGURE 2.2 Cost Management System

4. Quality and value improvement tools.
5. Implementation procedures.

A value-based cost management system can accomplish this by identifying the kinds of measures needed to establish the relationships between structures, processes, and outcomes on the one hand and quality, time, and cost on the other.

A patient-focused plan keeps the management of the costs of quality and value personal while identifying measures that are appropriate and useful for continuous improvement. Defining new cost categories in terms of patient satisfaction connects quality and value with financial results. These new categories, along with more-accurate cost information and the specific patient satisfaction definitions the organization develops, also clarify when incremental changes and when reengineering changes are appropriate. Tools and procedures for using the strategic plan and the cost-of-quality and value-added categories to achieve cost reductions by quality improvement help in making the cultural transformation that is needed by creating more skilled, experienced, and knowledgeable employees.

PATIENT-FOCUSED PLAN: HOW TO PROFIT FROM DELIVERY OF QUALITY HEALTHCARE SERVICES

The objective of a patient-focused strategic quality plan can be stated by one question: How can the organization profit by delivering quality healthcare services to all patients on time?[5] A patient-focused strategic quality plan for the individual, team, or organization consists of six elements: vision, mission, values, strategy, objectives, and measures. The need for the organization to have a patient-focused plan is obvious. However, as organizations are flattened and become more horizon-

5. Brown, Stephen W.; Nelson, Anne-Marie; Bronkesh, Sheryl J.; and Wood, Steven D. *Patient Satisfaction Pays: Quality Services for Practice Success.* Frederick, MD: Aspen Publishers, 1993.

tal, decision-making skills are required of employees at organizational levels unaccustomed to doing so. The use of a patient-focused plan helps all employees learn the necessary management skills for a horizontally-structured, process-oriented organization. Also, employees become better team members as measured by their contribution and support, the more skilled, experienced, and knowledgeable they are.

The patient-focused plan can be developed by answering the following questions:

- Vision—Where are we going?
- Mission—Who are we: market, product, service?
- Strategies—How will we get there?
- Objectives—How much will we do by when?
- Measures—How do we compare?
- Values—What do we stand for?

The six elements shown in the previous list can be grouped into two areas: the vision, mission, and values define the culture while the strategies, objectives, and measures define the operating plan. The purpose of the culture is to foster an environment conducive to continuous improvement of patient, employee, and business satisfaction. The operating plan states what the organization is to accomplish in the short term and what the priorities are for the limited resources available.

DEFINITION OF PATIENT SATISFACTION: HOW TO INCLUDE THE PATIENT IN YOUR PLANS

The definition of patient satisfaction determines the specific measures for improvement.[6] It links cost to quality and delivery so that cost reduction is possible through quality and de-

6. Leebov, Wendy. *Measuring and Managing Patient Satisfaction.* Chicago: American Hospital Publishing, Inc., 1993.

livery improvement. A patient-focused quality service meets or exceeds the patient's expectations. Juran distinguishes between two kinds of expectations for the purpose of connecting quality to costs.[7] Quality as an additional feature or added value is one type of expectation that usually adds to the cost and price of the service. Patients also expect defect-free service, or, what Juran calls freedom from deficiencies. Freedom from deficiencies is intimately tied to quality improvement through cost reduction. It is what Crosby refers to when speaking of zero defects.[8] It is what Deming refers to when stating that improving quality reduces costs because of less rework.[9] It is what connects quality and financial performance causally through the equation *income = revenues – expenses* because of fewer expenses as a result of less rework.

NEW EXPENSE CATEGORIES: HOW TO MANAGE COST SYSTEMS BASED ON QUALITY AND DELIVERY

The general ledger, income statement, and balance sheet traditionally provide three ways of collecting and analyzing financial and cost information. They each serve different purposes by arranging data to answer specific questions. These questions are concerned with the organization's profitability and viability:

- How did we do compared to what we expected (during a defined accounting period)?
- Where did a variance occur?
- What did it cost to deliver services?
- How much income did we earn for these services?

---

7. Juran, J.M. *Juran on Leadership for Quality.* New York: The Free Press, 1989, pp. 68–75.
8. Crosby, P.B. *Quality is Free.* New York: McGraw-Hill Book Company, 1984.
9. Deming, W.E. *Out of the Crisis.* Cambridge, MA: MIT Center for Advanced Engineering Study, 1986, pp. 1–3.

Compare these questions to some of those posed by the executive in chapter 1:

- What is the net profit or loss for each patient?
- What was the cost of poor quality and delivery of services to patients and employees?
- How can everyone reduce costs by improving quality and delivery?

The first set of questions fails to identify where the opportunities are for cost reductions through quality improvement because they do not include the patient or employee as a customer, they do not include quality, and they do not include delivery. The equations for the balance sheet and income statement are based on the *equity = assets – liabilities* and *net income = revenues – expenses* equations, neither of which includes quality, delivery, or patient and employee satisfaction.

New expenses categories—prevention, processing, appraisal, failure—called cost of quality (COQ),[10] however, allow you to answer these questions. Activity-based costing (ABC) is used to determine which cost objects are profitable, and value-added (VA) analysis helps in determining where there is inefficiency. These analyses can take general ledger items and analyze them in three steps: ABC to determine profits, VA analysis to address delivery, and COQ analysis to reduce the cost of quality (see Figure 2.3).

---

10. The earliest references to the idea of cost-of-quality and the creation of categories are: Juran, J.M. *Quality Control Handbook,* 1st Edition, McGraw-Hill, 1951 and Feigenbaum, A.V. *Total Quality Control,* McGraw-Hill, 1961, chapter 5. Since the early 1960s, numerous other publications illustrate the applicability of the concepts to a variety of manufacturing situations (e.g., Atkinson, Jr., J.H.; Hohmer, Gregory; Mundt, Barry; Troxel, Richard B.; and Whichell, William. *Current Trends in Cost of Quality.* Montvale, NJ: National Association of Accountants, 1991. More recently, the concepts have been successfully applied to service industries (e.g., Lawrence P. Carr, "Applying Cost of Quality to a Service Business," *Sloan Management Review,* Summer 1992, pp. 72–77.

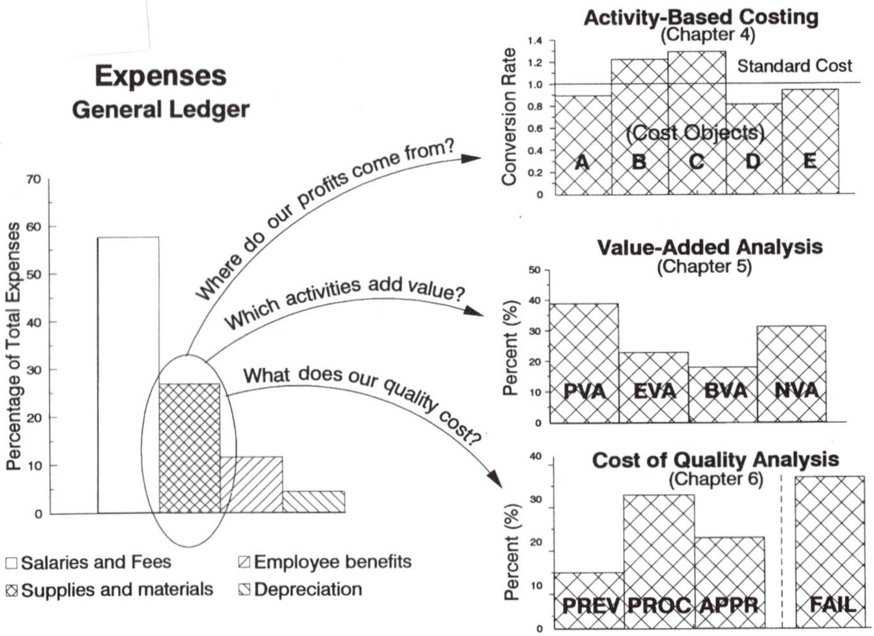

FIGURE 2.3 New Analyses to Achieve Better Cost Estimates and Include Value and Quality

QUALITY IMPROVEMENT TOOLS: HOW TO MAKE FACT-BASED DECISIONS

The quality improvement tools are used in the implementation procedures described in the following section. They address five key areas:

- Measures of quality, delivery, and cost: Pareto, bar, and run charts; surveys, interviews.
- Analyses of performance (clinical and operational): cause-and-effect and flow diagrams, brainstorming.
- Controls of services and processes: control and other charts and graphs, data collection procedures.
- Actions for correction: design of experiments, data collection, brainstorming, action plans, affinity diagrams.

- Systems for prevention: design of experiments, data collection, action plans, force field analysis.

Without tools, little or haphazard progress will be made in reducing costs and improving quality. Tools help in several ways:

- Deciding where to start.
- Defining processes, services, and products.
- Confirming the critical steps of processes.
- Identifying customers and suppliers.
- Discovering patient, customer, and your own needs.
- Identifying quality metrics.
- Discovering where, when, and what to measure.
- Estimating costs of quality.
- Developing causal explanations of dissatisfaction and nonconformance through root cause analysis.
- Defining problems or opportunities.
- Generating creative solutions.[11]

IMPLEMENTATION PROCEDURES: HOW TO USE THE VALUE-BASED COST MANAGEMENT SYSTEM

The purpose of establishing procedures for existing services is to identify ways of accomplishing more (higher quality and better delivery) while spending less (reducing costs), for exam-

11. There are several sources for descriptions of a variety of quality improvement tools: Growth Opportunity Alliance of Greater Lawrence. *The Memory Jogger. A Pocket Guide of Tools for Continuous Improvement:* G.O.A.L./QOC; also, Berwick, D.M., Godfrey, A.B., and Roessner, J. *Curing Health Care.* San Francisco: Jossey-Bass Publishers, 1991. Kelly, Michael R. *Everyone's Problem-Solving Handbook.* White Plains, NY: Quality Resources, Inc., 1992.

ple, how to admit or register patients more efficiently so their needs are addressed profitably. The purpose of establishing procedures for new services or programs is to identify ways of better meeting patient needs (higher quality and better delivery) more profitably (spending less), for example, developing a specialized procedure and intervention for battered women to prevent or reduce the number of repeat interventions.

You will need procedures in six areas:

1. To identify process activities: standard operating procedures for operational procedures and critical pathways for clinical procedures.
2. To evaluate the effectiveness, efficiency, and adaptability of all procedures.
3. To take corrective actions through problem solving with failures that have already occurred.
4. To take preventive actions through problem solving to eliminate or reduce failures.
5. To continuously improve through cost reductions by improvement of quality and value.
6. To implement the new quality-based cost management concepts.

OVERVIEW

Figure 2.4 describes the role of value-based cost management in the planning and day-to-day activities of the organization. It is also provides the framework for answering the senior executive's nine questions listed in chapter 1. In the remaining chapters, the ideas behind value-based cost management are described in greater detail and illustrated. In this chapter, you saw briefly how senior management could develop a strategic plan that was patient-focused.

Chapter 3 continues with the fundamental premise behind continuous improvement: processes. Activity-based

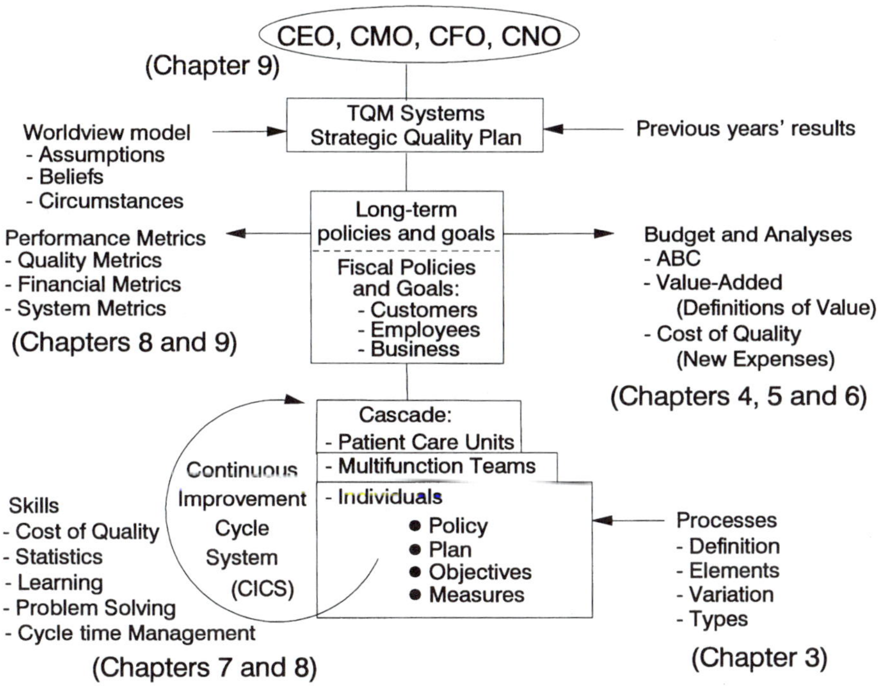

FIGURE 2.4 The Role of Value-Based Cost Management

costing, value-added analysis, and cost of quality are explained in chapters 4 through 6 to help answer the first five questions. In chapter 7, these elements are integrated into continuous improvement along with four other skills—statistics, problem solving, cycle time management, and learning—to form the continuous improvement cycle system (CICS). This chapter helps answer the senior executive's question about skills needed to reduce costs by improving quality and delivery.

Examples of how to apply these concepts and tools is shown in chapter 8, which help answer the question of how to reduce quality and delivery costs. Chapter 9 closes the loop by providing answers to the last two questions: justifying an organization's quality efforts and senior management's role.

3 Processes: The Key to Continuous Improvement

Processes are the key to continuous improvement for one reason: they are used repetitively. Being repetitive, they give you another chance to do better. The new healthcare management philosophies are based on the premise that everything you do is a process. That means you can continuously improve every aspect of the organization to design, develop, and deliver quality healthcare services.

WHAT IS A PROCESS?

A process is a series of actions taken to produce something. When you look at processes in your organization, they typically have these five features:

- A sequence of activities.
- That is *repeated*.
- That *consumes* resources.
- By *transforming* one thing to another.
- To *satisfy* customer needs.

Quality gurus have attempted to remove the blame of process failures from people by saying systems and processes account for 75 percent to 95 percent of the failures customers encounter. This is inaccurate in one sense: organizational processes are designed and developed by people. They are used by people. They serve people. When they fail, corrections are made by people. Only people can improve processes.

No customer likes to hear from an employee, "I can't do that because of our policy or system." The customer's attitude, and the correct one, is: "So, change it—and you can start right now." Unfortunately, organizations do not think about changing, let alone changing so swiftly. They are given the second chance to improve but rarely take it because the organization's culture is not one of continuous improvement. For example, patients have frequently complained about waiting time, yet months and years pass before many hospitals address this issue.

Continuous improvement requires repeatedly answering two questions (see Figure 3.1):

- Q1. What are the current quality, delivery, and cost levels?
- Q2. How can these levels be improved?

If you aren't asking the first question, it is almost impossible to answer the second. Patients will tell us that they have

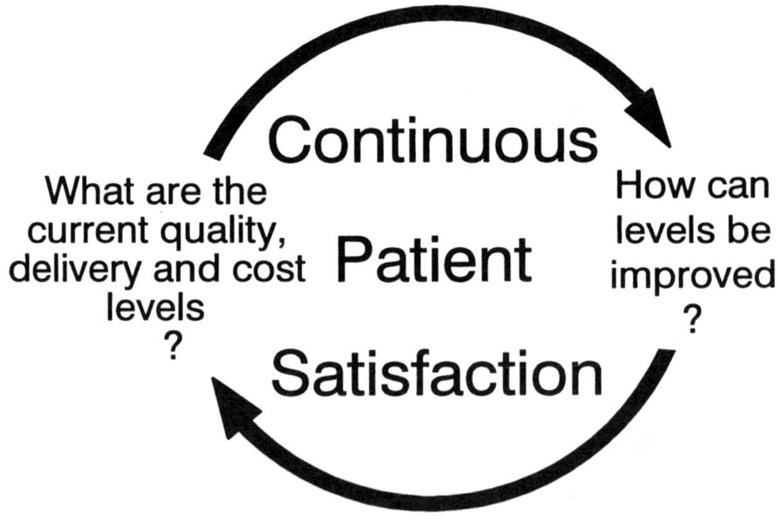

FIGURE 3.1 Continuous Improvement Cycle Questions

complained or offered suggestions. How many of these went left unheeded?

PROCESS ELEMENTS

All organizations have suppliers and customers (see Figure 3.2) and all processes consist of linkages between suppliers, processors, and customers (see Figure 3.3). The acronym SIPOC identifies the five process components: supplier-input-processor-output-customer. The central component is the processor, the person who does the transformation (e.g., a medical technologist tests a blood specimen to generate a report on the patient's cholesterol level). The processor starts with an input (i.e., the blood specimen and order) and transforms it to an output (i.e., the result on a report). Suppliers (i.e., phlebotomists, nurses, and clinicians) are the people who give the processor input (e.g., materials, supplies, and information). For example, the phlebotomist draws the blood and gives the medical technologist the specimen. The specific needs the output must meet are the needs of a customer. A customer is someone who depends on the output (e.g., the

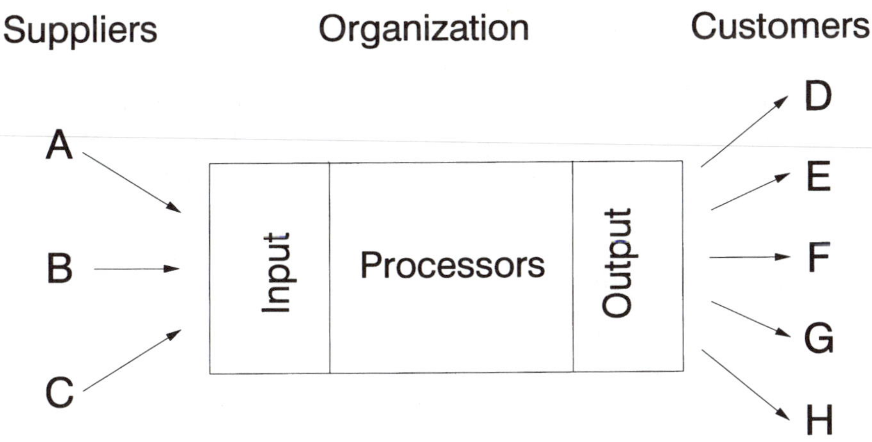

FIGURE 3.2 Process Elements

Supplier (name)	Input (list)	Processor (you)	Output (list)	Customer (name)
Administration Purchasing Ancillary Housekeeping	Support Services Supplies Materials	Nursing Units Patient-Care Units	Healthcare Services and Products	Patient

FIGURE 3.3 Linkages Between Process Elements

clinician to treat the patient and the patient to receive appropriate care).

Sometimes, quality efforts start by looking at the supplier-customer linkages and asking every employee to identify all their customers. The employees are then trained on quality tools and asked to start satisfying all their customers. In healthcare, this approach to quality will not work because it becomes too easy for the patient to get lost among all the other types of customers. A better perspective is to consider the healthcare organization as consisting of two groups of processes: those that serve the patient directly and those that support these processes. Because in healthcare the patient is the ultimate customer.

For example, critical pathways are processes because they describe the critical elements of care: input, procedures (transformations), and output.[1] They are likely to be patient-focused because they are formulated by a collaboration of health professionals: the processors and suppliers. They can be valuable for continuous improvement because they provide feedback that can be used to answer the two continuous improvement questions (Q1 and Q2) when coupled with data on the parameters of care and clinical outcomes.

1. Zander, K. "Nursing Case Management: Strategic Management of Cost and Quality Outcomes," *JONA* 1988:18(5):23–30.

PATIENT NEEDS AND SATISFACTION

The quality of the output is determined by the extent to which it satisfies the customer's needs, or in healthcare, patient satisfaction and the result of the clinical procedures. These needs are what the patient wants fulfilled. Satisfaction is a measure of that fulfillment. Open-ended questions can help identify needs, while scales measure satisfaction. For example, asking "What did you like about . . . ?" or "What would you change about . . . ?" are questions more likely to reveal the patient's specific needs and priorities. On the other hand, asking "How would you rate our . . . [poor, marginal, acceptable, good, excellent]?" may reveal high satisfaction with an aspect of service that is irrelevant or inconsequential when it is not derived from the previous types of questions or solicitations.[2]

The task in increasing satisfaction is in identifying the needs, translating them to specifications for or characteristics of the output, and then measuring the extent to which those characteristics address the need. For example, a patient need may be to have courteous healthcare professionals. Unfortunately, because satisfaction is a measure of the product or service fulfilling the needs, it is not readily discernable to the processor. For one patient, courtesy may mean addressing them by their name, while to another it may mean respecting their privacy. Therefore determining what courtesy means to patients may require asking them individually before criteria can be specified. Often, processors merely measure the product or service characteristics, which may not be correlated with customer satisfaction. So, courtesy may be measured or felt to be addressed by the number of times or the length of time the staff interacts with the patient. A lack of interaction may be viewed as impolite by some patients. Certainly, it is easier to measure time and occurrences. It is also easier to focus on your own needs because you are so aware of them.

---

2. Leebov, Wendy. *Service Excellence: The Customer Relations Strategy for Health Care.* Chicago: American Hospital Publishing, Inc., 1988.

The National Demonstration Project (NDP) for Quality Improvement in Health Care, in which the University of Michigan Medical Center participated, showed that the general principles of the industrial quality model were applicable to healthcare. However, a disappointment mentioned by Berwick and Godfrey was that "Not a single NDP team [of the 17 healthcare organizations who participated] measured its success in terms of improved health status of patients."[3] This was consistent with the Ernst & Young and the American Quality Foundation Study. It reported that less than 26 percent of hospitals used customer complaints as their major or primary source for new products and services. In addition, another survey of more than 3,000 hospitals conducted as part of a grant from The Baxter Foundation indicated that while 7 in 10 were TQM/CQI facilities by their own classification, there was no difference in patient care outcomes between the quality facilities and the non-quality facilities.

Despite these results, there has been a recent flurry of concepts and approaches to delivering healthcare and restructuring to focus on the patient. Patient satisfaction can be broadly classified under three areas:

- Quality: meeting clinical and personal expectations and needs.
- Delivery: timeliness of and access to service.
- Cost: price.[4]

Clinical satisfaction comes from clinical intervention: prevention, screening, diagnostic, therapeutic and other management procedures to cure or ameliorate a health care issue and

3. Berwick, D.M.; Godfrey, A.B.; and Roessner, J. *Curing Health Care.* San Francisco: Jossey-Bass Publishers, 1991.

4. Shigeru, Mizuno. *Company-Wide Total Quality Control 2nd ed.* Tokyo: Asian Productivity Organization (distributed by Quality Resources), 1989, pp. 338–339.

the management of failures, e.g., readmissions and reoperations. Operational satisfaction includes patient satisfaction and interactions between patient and employees (medical, support, business).[5]

Nonconformances are failures to meet patient needs because a patient-desired characteristic or outcome is lacking or a non-desired characteristic or outcome exists. Quality measures are scales that measure nonconformance per unit (e.g., service or person), the number of units with nonconformance, or levels of patient/customer dissatisfaction. Examples of measures of quality indicative of nonconformance include unnecessary or preventable:

- Delays in admission and healthcare delivery.
- Surgeries.
- Lengths of stay (LOS).
- Morbidities.
- Mortalities.
- Readmissions.

These are expressed as the per number of patients or number of patient days. These types of nonconformance relate to the clinical outcome of the health service provided.

In addition, the manner and appearance of the healthcare professional play a critical role in patient satisfaction.[6] Patient satisfaction surveys often report that attention, concerns, and demeanor of the staff and medical provider are top factors in patient satisfaction. For example, Press Ganey Associates of

5. Holloway, James J. and Thomas J. William, "Measuring the Quality of Care Received by Elderly Patients," in *Quality and Cost Containment in Care of the Elderly* (eds) James C. Romers, Rodney M. Coe. New York: Springer Publishing Co., 1991, chapter 6.

6. Cunningham, L. *The Quality Connection in Health Care.* San Francisco: Jossey-Bass Publishers, 1991, pp. 13–32.

Indiana reported that the 14 most important factors for patients had nothing to do with the technical skill of the healthcare providers or the adequacy of the equipment and instrumentation. Words used by patients to indicate what their needs from healthcare providers were: concern, sensitivity, cheerfulness, attitude, courtesy, friendliness, and communicative.

Delivery refers to the effective use of time—that is,

- Appropriate frequency of clinical and operational intervention.
- Accessibility.
- Turnaround and cycle-time.
- Throughput or volume.
- Flexibility and adaptability.

Cost is an issue for both the patient and the organization because of the links between the patient's quality perspective and the organization's cost perspective. The organization separates its functions typically into revenue centers and nonrevenue or cost centers. Revenue centers are those that produce revenues through clinical processes (e.g., surgery, physical therapy, and the emergency department). Cost centers are those whose expenses are indirectly distributed to the revenue centers by averaging across volume. Cost centers (e.g., accounts payable, scheduling, medical records, billing, and laundry) impact patient satisfaction directly on the operational side of quality. They also affect the clinical side by causing delays and consuming nonclinical resources.

Traditionally, quality, cost, and delivery are viewed as opposing forces, each giving way to the other: to improve quality, costs must increase or delivery worsen; and vice-versa. However, improving delivery (reducing the time to deliver services) or reducing deficiencies creates increased capacity. Since costs are typically based on volume, increased capacity allows for increased volume, which in turn can reduce costs per unit of service. With hospitals competing for a variety of managed care contracts on price per member, improved quality and delivery (increased patient satisfaction) offer a way to be more competitive.

OVERVIEW

Process variation is the nemesis of quality. Processes vary in their quality, delivery, and cost. There are numerous reasons for these variations: variations in suppliers and their input, variations in procedures for the same process, variations in output. Figure 3.4 provides a generic overview of the clinical process and its two subprocesses—diagnostic and therapeutic—patient presents with a clinical problem or complaint that is clinically diagnosed and followed by intervention resulting in an outcome. There are variations in patients, how they enter the clinical process, the diagnostic procedures, the decision for intervention, the intervention, the outcomes, and the therapeutic procedures. The surprise is not that there are differences, but that there is such a large degree of successful healthcare delivery given the numerous areas for variation (see Table 3.1).

The result is variation in patient outcomes:

- Different mortality, morbidity, readmission, and functionality rates (clinical quality).
- Different patient satisfaction, employee morale, and productivity levels (operational quality).
- Different lengths of stay (delivery).
- Different degrees of accessibility (delivery).
- Different net revenues (cost).

The medical literature contains several hundred articles on variations in healthcare practices. While the initial reac-

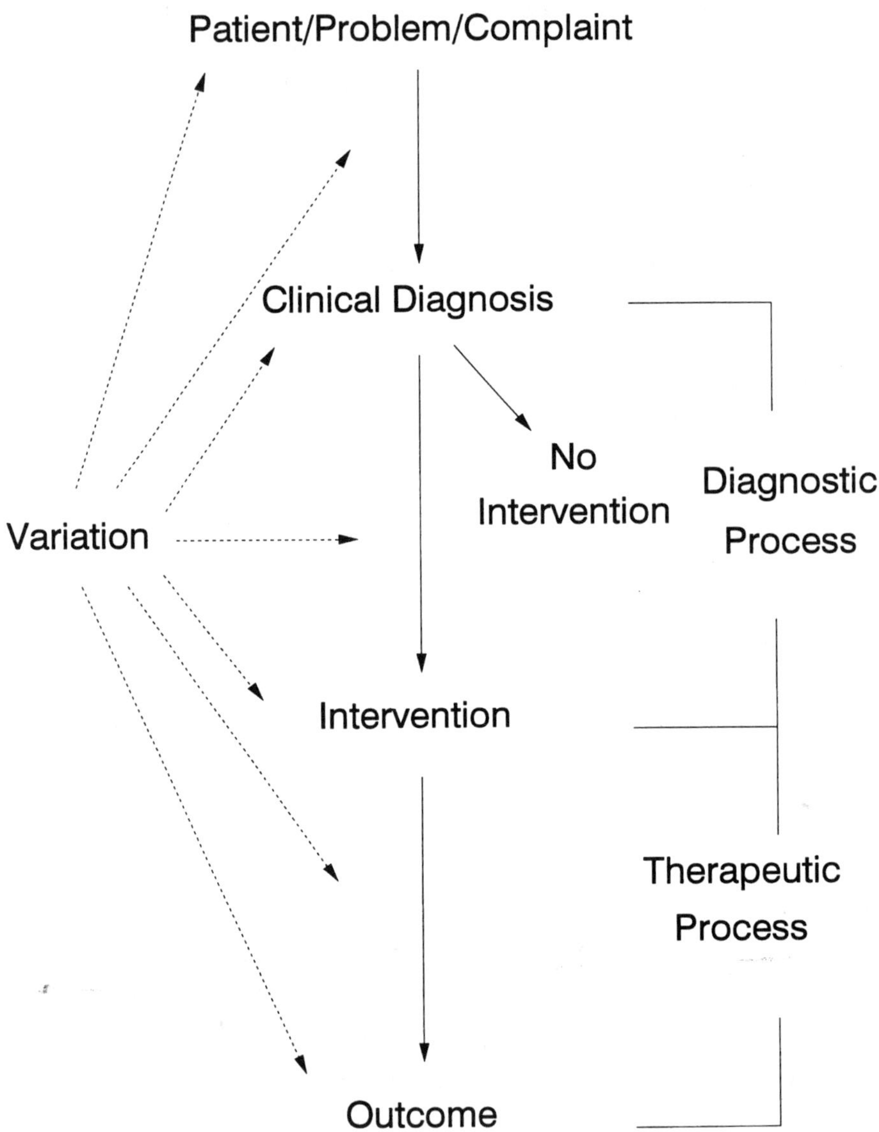

FIGURE 3.4 The Clinical Process

TABLE 3.1. Sources of Variation in Healthcare Processes

Patients	Provider*	Intervention	Cost	Revenue	Outcomes
• Demographics • Degree of morbidity • Degree of co-morbidities • Lifestyle	• Diagnosis • Treatment • Cycle-time • Skills • Systems • Physical layout • Resources • Set-ups • Preparations • Application of technical procedures • Reaction time when things go wrong • Staffing levels and skills • Medications	• Physical practice patterns • Details of physician documentation of care • Skill levels of medical record coders • Risk selection	• Uniformity in reporting • Component costs • Complications • Medication regimens • Reporting of surgeon fees • Charge structure • Utilization of resources • Risk selection • Modality	• Blue Cross • Medicare • Medicaid • Commercial insurer • Self-payer	• Mortality • Morbidity • Readmissions • Functionality • Patient satisfaction • Employee morale • Productivity • Accessibility • Delivery • Net revenues

*Sloan, Frank A; Blumstein, James F; and Perren, James M., Eds. *Cost, Quality, and Access in Health Care for the Elderly*. San Francisco: Jossey-Bass Publishers, 1988, pp. 125–140.

tion is to discount such variations because of mitigating factors, these studies controlled for these differences in their analyses, and the variations still exist. These variations occur not only in what healthcare organizations can control to some extent (e.g., quality, delivery, and costs), but also in what may be beyond their control (e.g., regulations, suppliers, and insurers).

Even today, most healthcare providers do not know what these variations are within their own organization, why they occur, or how to reduce them, and these variations and their causes do not reveal themselves in the profit-and-loss statement looked at by the executive in chapter 1. Before you can make improvements, however, you need to be aware of the variation, accurately measure the effect of the variation, and identify the sources of the variation in quality, delivery, and cost.

4 Activity-Based Costing

Accurate estimates of costs are critical for the successful reduction in variation of quality and delivery to be cost-effective. This chapter examines different ways of estimating costs, what is required to estimate them more accurately, and how to balance the cost of obtaining accurate information with the value it provides in decision making. This information provides answers to the first two questions raised by the executive in chapter 1: Are the cost estimates accurate? What is the net profit or loss for each patient?

STANDARD COSTS

All costs are estimated by averaging. The average cost overestimates some applications and underestimates others. Nevertheless, if the differences are not too great, the estimates are useful. The question in estimating costs is: Can I find an average that is easy and inexpensive to determine yet accurate enough for my application?

In determining various costs associated with a patient, traditional cost accounting uses standard costs based on averages of direct resources consumed. These averages consist of finding a group of resources that are similar in cost and averaging their total cost over a set period of time. For example, if we pay a nurse $25 an hour and over a period of six months she spends on average four hours per patient per day, we can establish a standard cost of $100 per patient per day in direct nursing costs. Indirect resources are averaged and estimated as a percent of the direct costs, typically based on volume. If during the six months, administrative, clerical, and other overhead costs represented 13 percent of the direct costs, the total direct and indirect costs would be: \$100 + (13% of \$100) = \$113.[1]

Suppose a nursing unit consists of three registered nurses (RNs), two licensed practical nurses (LPNs), and one nurse assistant (NA), or six nursing employees. During a three-month period, the number of nursing hours spent per patient day is estimated to be 4.8 across all patients. Because the different nursing levels have different salaries, an average nursing salary is determined in proportion to the number of nurses of each level. So, 3⁄6 of the average RN hourly rate plus 2⁄6 of the average LPN hourly rate plus 1⁄6 of the NA hourly rate yields an average nursing hourly rate. This is multiplied by the number of nursing hours per patient day to get an average nursing cost per patient day. Benefits and coverage costs are also averaged and added to the nursing costs as a percentage of the nursing hourly rate. This is called a direct cost. A similar analysis is used for indirect nursing and non-nursing care costs (e.g., ancillary costs, room bed—see Figure 4.1). These costs are standardized as a percentage of the average direct hourly nursing costs during the same period.

While standard costs are averages because there are variations, their use, as in hospitals today, is based on the assumption that all patients see the same hospital resources in the same proportion they occur in the unit, or over some period of time, the average for all patients would be the same as the standard cost. That is, all patients of the same type, such as by Diagnostic-Related Groups (DRG) severity classification, are charged according to the standard cost. This means, in the previous example, that each patient is assumed to have needed or consumed exactly 4.8 hours of nursing and exactly:

- 2.4 (= 3⁄6 of 4.8) hours of RN nursing.
- 1.6 (= 2⁄6 of 4.8) hours of LPN nursing.
- 0.8 (= 1⁄6 of 4.8) hours of NA nursing.

1. Omachonu, V.K. *Total Quality and Productivity Management in Health Care Organizations.* Milwaukee: ASQC, 1991.

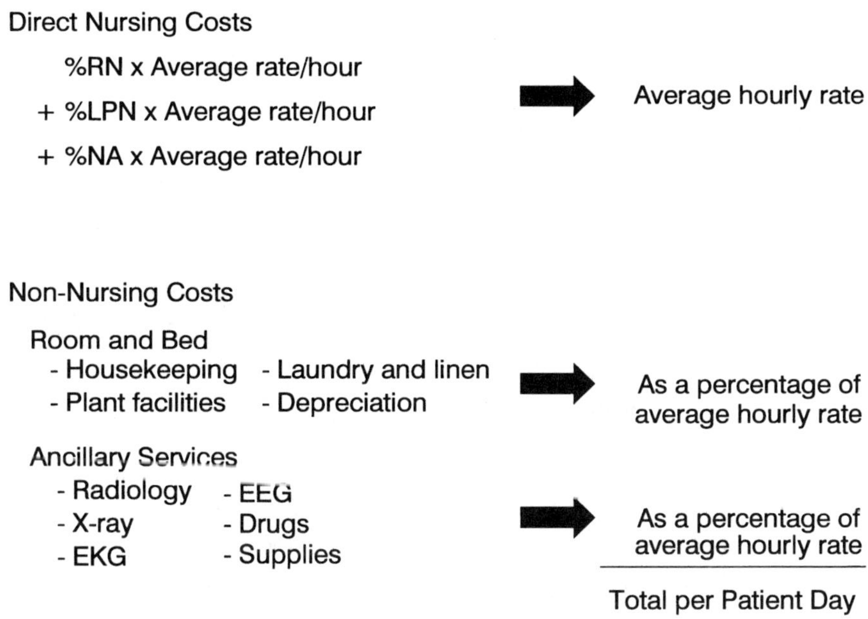

FIGURE 4.1 Analysis of Direct Nursing and Non-Nursing Costs

Total average charges will include, for example, an additional 13.2 percent of their charges for such ancillary services as radiology, supplies, X-rays, EKG, pharmacy, and so on.

CONSEQUENCES OF INACCURACY

The financial picture looks quite different when viewed in the aggregate. Aggregate information is useful (when comprehensive and includes additional information) for assessing long-term progress. It won't, however, tell you of significant changes in day-to-day activities. The reason is that while expenses are averaged for standard costs, actual revenues and quality are determined individually (see Figure 4.2).

A simple example illustrates the issue. Suppose that for the last three months the aggregate financial analysis of DRG 79 (respiratory infection) shows it has been profitable. It would appear from the aggregate data that no further analysis would be useful. However, if more accurate cost estimates

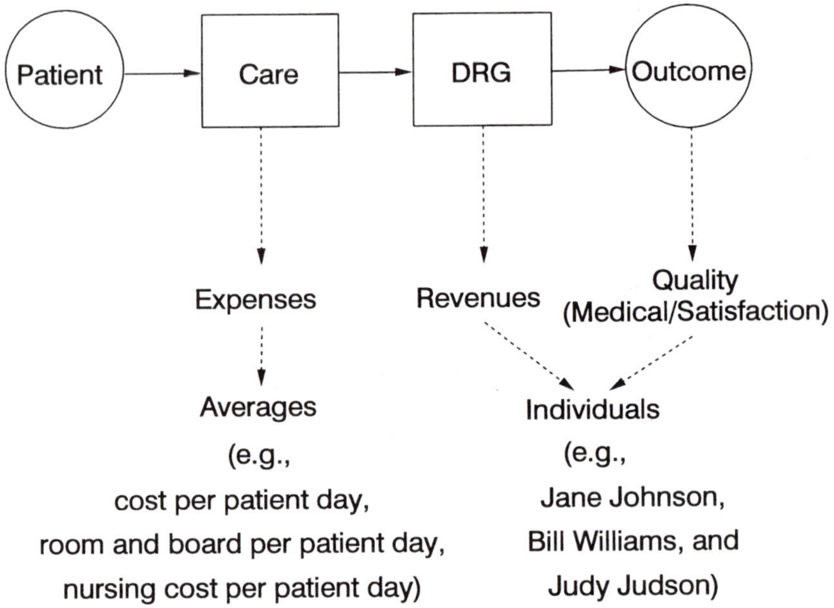

FIGURE 4.2 Expense Measurements Compared with Revenue and Quality Measurements

at the individual patient level were available, it may turn out that, say, 15 percent of the patients had an extended length of stay. This because of malnutrition that, if identified before intervention for respiratory infection, would be preventable. Because of the extended length of stay, these patients were actually treated at a loss. Fortunately, these patients were a small enough percentage of all DRG 79 patients so the losses were more than compensated by the patients that were profitable.

If the percentage of the types of patient who were susceptible to malnutrition increased during the next three months, the hospital could incur a net loss across all DRG 79 patients. The aggregate data would not reveal why—only that the profit picture had changed. Senior management would use the aggregate data to say that *on the average* DRG 79 patients had a net gain or loss. Without the accurate data at the individual level, they may make changes that have nothing to do with the *type* of patient. This would not only prolong the losses, but could make the losses even greater because the wrong problem was solved.

The purpose of improving costing is to have more accurate information for decision making. The standard cost approach described for nursing has another weakness. Even if the cost estimates are accurate, they do not provide clues for quality and delivery improvement because there is a separation of quality and delivery from productivity. Since the ratios and averages depend on volume for many cases, volumes can increase, making productivity better without any change in or a worsening of quality and delivery. The financial impact of this can go undetected. For example, an RN charges $25/hour or $250 for a 10-hour shift. If she attends three patients, the direct nursing costs are $83.33 per patient. If she attends four patients, they are $50 per patient. Getting more accurate information requires a different method for allocating costs.

SEQUENCE OF ACTIVITIES

In reality, because processes vary, not only will different types of patients (e.g., by DRG) vary in the proportion of nursing care used, but patients with the same DRG will also vary in the proportion of ancillary resources they use. The assumption for averaging is that the average will not differ significantly from the individual costs making up the average. If this assumption is true, the standard average cost will be useful for making management decisions because it will be accurate enough.

Unfortunately, it is not always possible to say beforehand how much accuracy is necessary. Because getting more information and more accurate information also costs money and consumes resources, there has to be a trade-off between the accuracy of the cost information and the cost of obtaining it. This is: Are there situations in your organization where standard costs are too inaccurate for the kinds of decisions you are making? For example, how much would you spend to increase the accuracy of the information on acute myocardial infarction patients if it had saved $1 million in losses?

To provide better estimates of the cost per patient, cost accounting must consider the actual resources used. Resources are consumed by the sequence of activities involved in carrying out processes. By more accurately identifying the activities and their costs, more accurate cost information is obtained. However, defining too minute activities results in unnecessary detail that is too costly to obtain.

The goal is to obtain just enough accuracy, relatively inexpensively, to show the connection between patient satisfaction and the bottom line. Patient-focused cost information should:

- Reveal sources of profit by patient-event or intervention.
- Be economical to obtain.
- Identify opportunities for improvement.
- Provide useful information for improvement and prevention.[2]

Activity-based costing (ABC) meets these requirements because it is based on these three principles:

1. Costs are assigned to cost objects.
2. Costs are assigned to activities triggered by cost objects.
3. The cost system must indicate what information is needed, how to extract it, and why it is needed.[3]

---

2. Turrey, Peter B.B. *Common Cents.* Hillsboro, OR: Cost Tech., 1991, p. 45.

3. Cooper R.; Kaplan, R.S.; Maisel, L.S.; Morrissey, E.; and Oehm, R.M. *Implementing Activity-Based Cost Management: Moving from Analysis to Action.* Montvale, NJ: Institute of Management Accountants, 1992. Also, O'Guin, Michael C. *The Complete Guide to Activity Based Costing.* Englewood Cliffs: Prentice Hall, 1991; Ostrenga, Michael R.; Ozan, Terrence R.; McIlhattan, Robert D.; and Harwood, Marcus D. *The Ernst & Young Guide to Total Cost Management.* New York: John Wiley & Sons, 1992.

Together, these three principles help us understand resource consumption from two perspectives: cost and process. These two perspectives provide information on profits; each is discussed in the following sections.

Cost perspective

Cost objects are the reasons for performing activities because they create a demand for activities (see dashed arrows, Figure 4.3). Activities in turn create a demand for resources. Resources create costs. Getting more accurate cost information is possible by reversing the demand flow to assign costs (solid arrows in Fig. 4.3).

Services, patients, and projects are cost objects because they create demands for activities that require resources. An

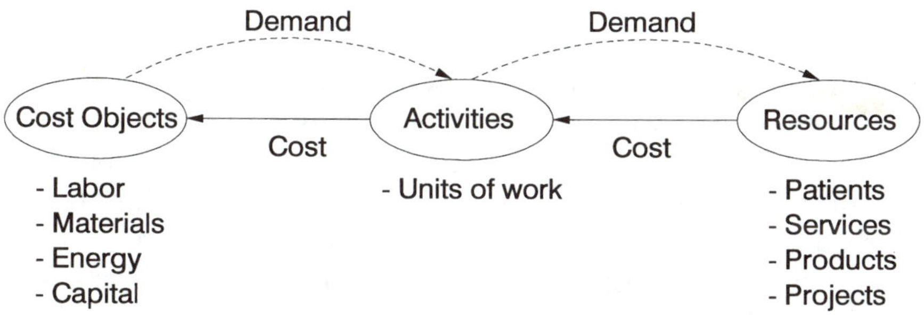

For example:

Patients with:
- GI carcinoma
- Burns
- Renal failure

Patients requiring resections:
- Colorectal
- Intestinal
- Gastro/esophageal

- Preoperative care
- Surgery
- Postoperative care
- Discharge assessment
- Billing

- Surgery labor, materials, supplies
- Food
- Drugs
- Nursing labor
- Room
- Energy
- Equipment

FIGURE 4.3 Demand Flow versus Cost Flow

activity is a unit of work (e.g., nursing, surgery, or physical therapy). The more specific the activity, the more accurate the cost information will be. However, it typically costs more to collect and analyze data at a more detailed level. Patients with renal failure trigger a list of activities defined by the critical pathway or procedure—preoperative care, surgery, postoperative care, discharge assessment, billing. These activities then require the use of resources (e.g., labor, supplies, materials, equipment, and capital).

This perspective differs from traditional cost assignments and Medicare approaches. These approaches assign costs to cost pools (e.g., nonrevenue centers), which are then allocated proportionally to the revenue centers. By assigning resources to activities, which in turn are assigned to the output or cost objects, more accurate cost estimates are possible. For example, the patient in Figure 4.3 requiring a colorectal resection creates a demand for postoperative care that in turn creates a demand for nursing labor. By assigning the specific nursing labor to the postoperative care for the specific patient, the expenses for that patient can be estimated more accurately.

A managerial advantage is that tracking resources to activities changes the traditional focus from inventory valuation to valuation of resources. For example, rather than incurring non-value-added expenses on large inventories, those costs could be expended on better resource use because of more accurate cost estimates. Because the primary cost object in healthcare is the patient, this approach to costing fits well with the current focus on outcomes. The resources used can be valued with respect to the contribution they make to desirable patient outcomes.

Process perspective

As shown in Figure 4.4, cost drivers are defined by answering the question: Why do we have this workload? Cost drivers

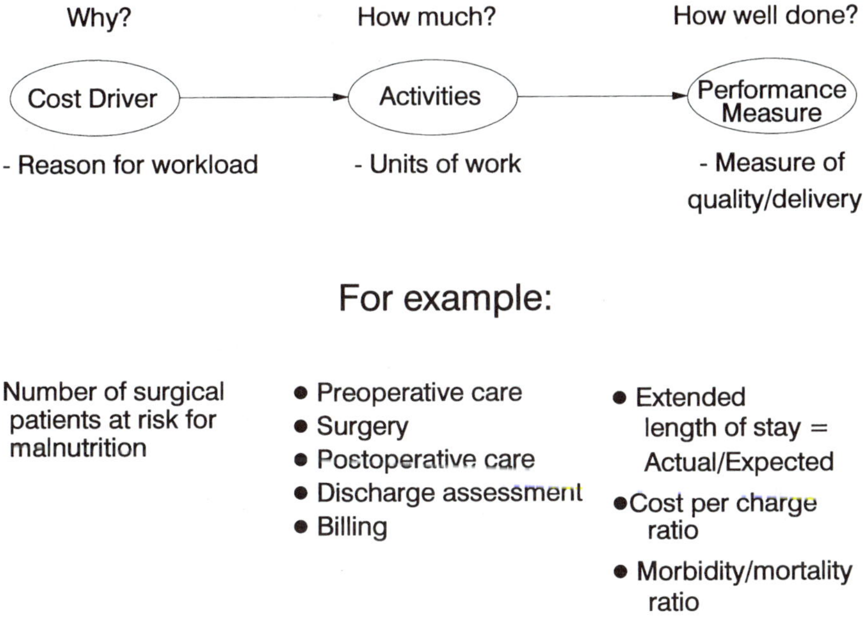

FIGURE 4.4 Cost Drivers

tell us why there is demand for activities (e.g., the number of surgical patients at risk for malnutrition). This determines how much activity is needed (i.e., how many units of work). Activities in turn tell us how much effort is required or how many resources are used. The effectiveness of this activity is evaluated by performance measures. Performance measures answer the question: How well were the activities performed? The answer to this question provides measures of quality and delivery. For example, the effectiveness of activities needed to meet the workload of some number of surgical patients at risk for malnutrition can be measured by the number of extended lengths of stay, cost/charge ratios, and morbidity/mortality ratios.

Cost drivers cause expenses to be incurred. As their volume increases, the costs increase (see Figure 4.5). For example, pharmacy costs are driven by the cost of drugs, the number of patient days, and the number of pharmacist's

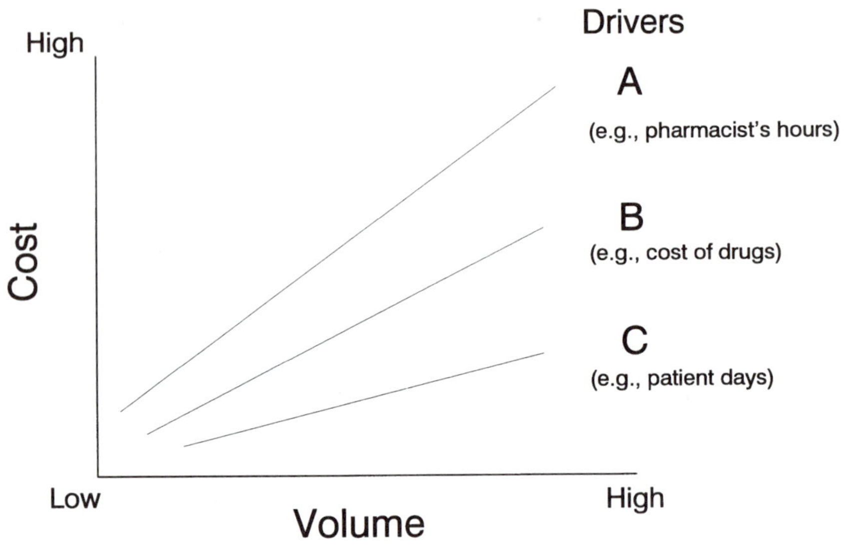

FIGURE 4.5 Relationship of Volume of Drivers to Cost

hours.[4] Each of these drivers has an impact on total pharmacy costs. The relationship between the volume of these drivers and the cost is stronger relatively speaking if the slopes of this relationship are steeper. Thus, cost driver A (pharmacist's hours) is the best driver to use with respect to accuracy because it is relatively more sensitive to changes in volume. Cost driver C (say, patient days) is the relatively least sensitive of the three drivers. A more sensitive driver detects changes in the averages more quickly, so management is alerted sooner and can respond quicker.

Traditionally, hospitals use the cost of drugs as a driver. Certainly, it is true that as more drugs are used, the total cost of pharmacy increases. The causal connection is evident. Using this cost driver, traditional costing determines the total cost for a drug, adds an allocated indirect cost based on the volume, and then divides this combined cost by the number

4. Finkler, Steven A. *Issues in Cost Accounting for Health Care Organizations.* Gaithersburg, MD: Aspen Publishers, Inc., 1993, Part IV.

of doses dispensed. This may be sufficiently accurate if the labor cost per dose is small compared to the cost of the drug.

The pharmacist also dispenses total parenteral nutrition (TPN) solutions. If the standard cost is based on volume for pills and TPN, labor (pharmacist's hours) is distributed proportionally to pills and TPN. This may be accurate for the pills but would not be accurate for TPN because the labor involved for preparing TPN solutions is far greater than for pills. What really drives the cost of TPN is labor. The standard cost based on volume may be off 50 percent to 100 percent compared to the cost estimated using ABC. Is it worth using different cost drivers or switching to ABC for pharmacy? The answer depends on the cost-driver volume and the kind of decision to be made.

Performance measures indicate how well the activities achieved their objective. Quality and delivery measures can be used to evaluate how well the effort succeeded in meeting the needs of the patient. For example, each DRG has an expected length of stay (LOS). The ratio of the actual LOS to the expected LOS is one measure of the performance of a DRG-specific process to trigger activities and the use of resources appropriate for that patient. A driver for these activities and the performance measure could be the number of DRG-specific patients admitted.

PROFIT INFORMATION

With ABC, a better estimate of actual costs is made at the level at which cost objects are defined. If a cost object is a DRG, the use of standard costs will say that all patients charged to that DRG yielded the same net profit to the provider. However, examining different classes of patients under the same DRG or each patient individually shows that the net profit will vary by patient (again, otherwise why take an average and not just collect data on the first or any one patient charged to that DRG?). ABC shows which cost objects were profitable and which were not when compared to the standard cost approach (see Figure 4.6). The standard cost will be the same for a group of cost objects, say patients A through E with the same DRG at the same acuity level, because they are used to create the average cost for that standard. Because there are variations between cost objects, the average will underestimate some and overestimate others.

If the census for these types of patients changes over the next period, the standard cost should be adjusted. More important, the standard cost may miss identifying opportunities for improvement by not recognizing that patients B and D were actually profitable while the others were not.

For example, five patients A through E admitted for simple pneumonia will receive reimbursement under DRG 89. Each will trigger a set of activities that in turn trigger the use of resources: labor, energy, material, and capital. The hospital incurs expenses with the consumption of these resources. There are many reasons (see chapter 2) these five patients will

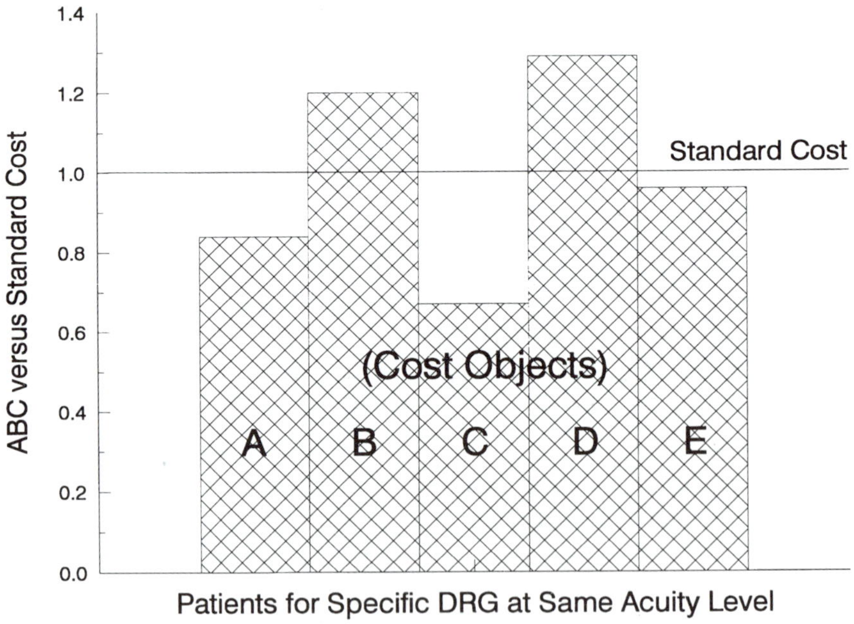

FIGURE 4.6 ABC versus Standard Cost Estimates

not consume the same amount of resources: they will need different amounts of nursing, food, antibiotics, and so on. The net profit for each will vary, even if the hospital receives the same reimbursement of $2,082.

The total aggregate profitability is five times $2,082 minus the total expenses (see Figure 4.7). From the individual expenses of each patient, clearly the hospital was profitable overall with only one patient yielding a loss. If this type of patient occurred more frequently relative to the other types of patients, total profits would decrease.

The cost of tracking costs assigned to cost objects depends on the method of accounting for resources consumed and the ease with which the data can be collected and stored. Traditional cost accounting already creates accounts by departments, projects, DRGs, and so on. With today's computer technology, data collection can be economical without being intrusive. By applying the Pareto principal of looking for the critical few areas that account for most of the costs, ABC can be applied in particular areas rather than attempting to replace the current cost-accounting system.

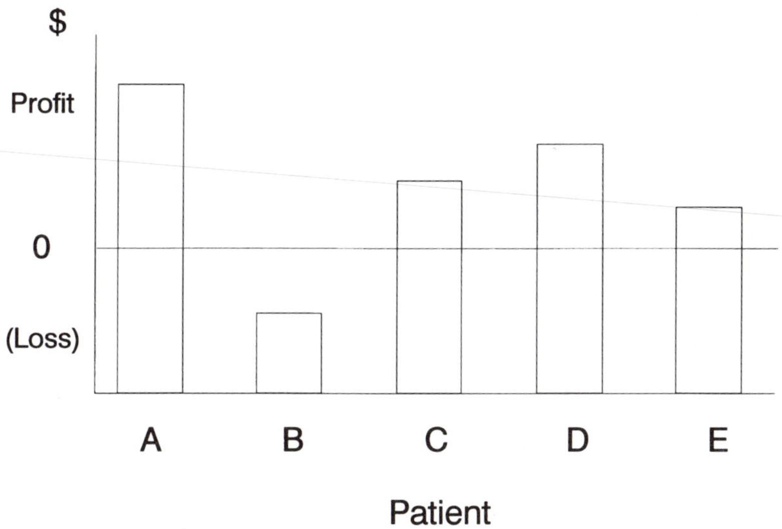

FIGURE 4.7 Total Aggregate Profitability

The major advantage of ABC is that by having more accurate estimates of costs at the cost object level, there is a better chance to reduce variation because the data are closer to the root cause of the variation. The information at the cost object level is more useful for improvement and prevention activities. For example, reasons for nonconformance to accepted practices (e.g., diagnostic failures for epileptic patients—see Figure 4.8) occur at the cost object level. Corrective action (e.g., additional care) results in increased but preventable costs. If these costs are not reimbursable, the net profit on that cost object will be less than expected. Cost objects that appear more profitable using ABC than standard costs are prime targets for improvement.

OVERVIEW

In summary, activity-based costing can provide more accurate cost estimates at a level of detail that is more useful for

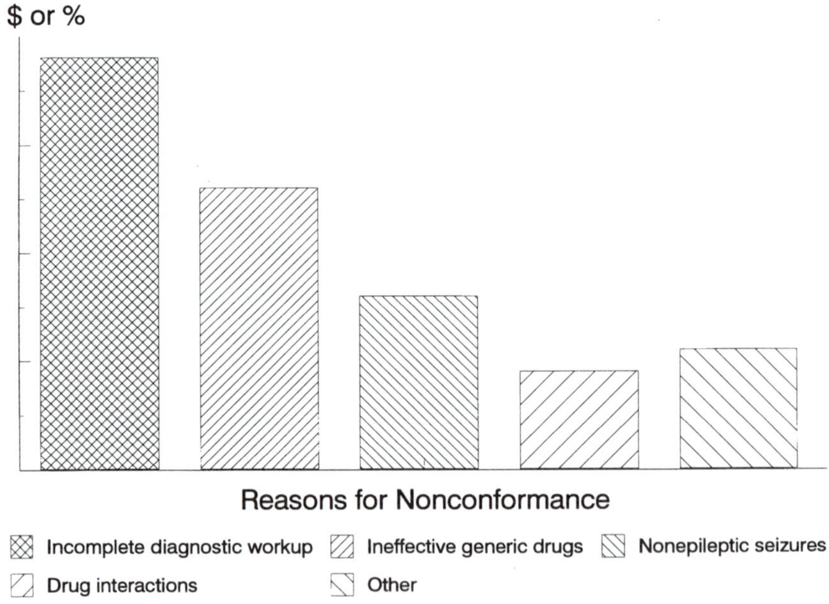

FIGURE 4.8 Diagnostic Failures for Epileptic Patients

continuous improvement. More accurate cost estimates allow management to more accurately answer the question "Where do our profits come from?" With this information, management can take steps to maintain profitable services and product lines. Unprofitable services and product lines can either be improved or, in the current alliance and consolidation environment, be used to trade with other healthcare organizations.

5 Value-Added Analysis

Should management choose to improve any of its service or product lines after determining more accurately which ones were profitable and which ones were not, additional analyses are required. The next analysis is to determine as quickly as possible which aspects of these service or product processes can be eliminated. This analysis, called value-added analysis (VA), helps the executive in chapter 1 answer the question "Which activities added value to the patient, employee, and the business?"

VALUE-ADDED DEFINITIONS

When cost objects trigger a demand for activities, resources are consumed. Patients are cost objects. They trigger a demand for activities that consume resources. While each resource consumed incurs an expense, it is not true that each resource consumed helps the patient or is reimbursed. For example, a repeated X-ray is not reimbursed while the first (defective) X-ray adds no value to the patient's outcome or satisfaction. The use of these resources determines whether patient needs are met. The patient's diagnosis triggers a demand for activities that require the use of the hospital's resources to meet the patient's needs clinically and operationally.

The entire sequence of activities is a process. Processes are designed to add value to input through the transformation (see Figure 5.1). Ideally, the input to the work process is of high quality and arrives on time. The TQM assumption is

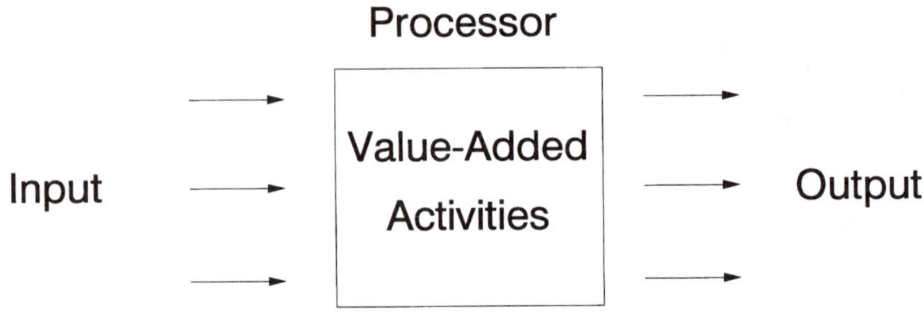

FIGURE 5.1 Process Design

that this can be achieved at costs that permit the organization to make a profit. In reality, the processing activities consist of both value-added activities and non-value-added (NVA) activities.[1] Examples of NVA activities are inspections, moving, queuing, storing, and waiting.

In considering the organizational Supplier-Input-Processor-Output-Customer (SIPOC) model, three entities are identifiable: the organization and associated stakeholders, the employees, and the patients (and communities). The purpose of TQM is to ensure that all three receive value. For this to occur, three types of processes must be identified: business value-added (BVA), employee value-added (EVA), and patient value-added (PVA). In Figure 5.2, these processes are listed in order of priority according to TQM. However, the order in which the value is added is reversed: the business must add value to the employee so the employee can add value to the patient.

PVA processes are necessary to meet the patient's requirements clinically and operationally (e.g., appropriate physician intervention and use of diagnostics).

EVA processes, activities and resources meet the employee's needs for job-satisfaction, development, and well-being. Examples of EVA activities include programs designed

1. Harrington, H.J. *Business Process Improvement.* New York: McGraw-Hill, Inc., 1991, chap. 6.

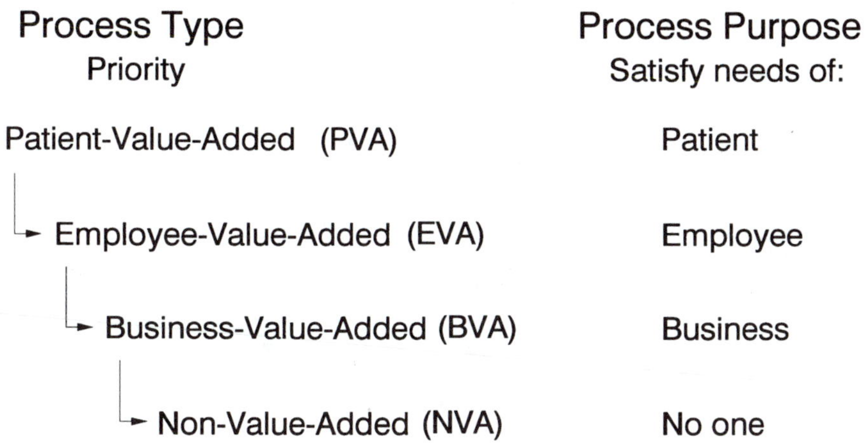

FIGURE 5.2 Process Priority According to TQM

to improve employee morale, safety, well-being, and satisfaction. Since employee productivity drives patient-value, it is critical that the organization identify, support, and continuously improve EVA processes. Improving EVA processes requires measuring productivity, loyalty, and job-satisfaction in terms of quality and PVA.

BVA processes depend on the success of the PVA and EVA processes to meet their objectives (e.g., financial analyses and fund-raising). Quality philosophies are based on the premise that profitability and market share result from successful efforts to increase the value of products and services provided to customers and employees.

All remaining processes are non-value-added (NVA). From the patient's perspective, waiting is an activity that does not meet his or her needs—that is, it does not add value (see Figure 5.3).

For example, a patient arriving at admissions may go through several steps (as shown in Figure 5.4):

1. Arrive and inform the admission's clerk.
2. Answer questions and fill out forms.

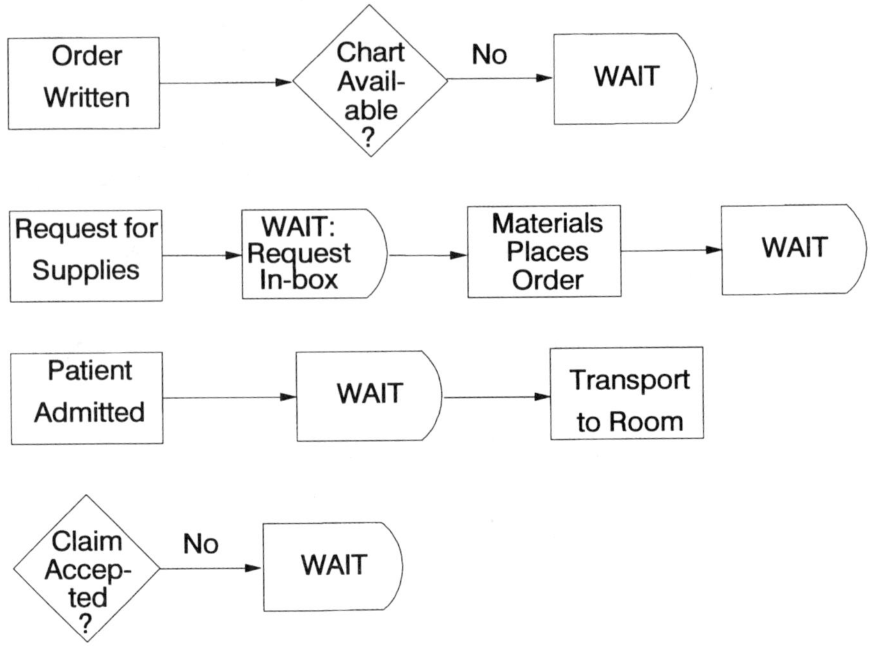

FIGURE 5.3 Non-Value-Added Processes

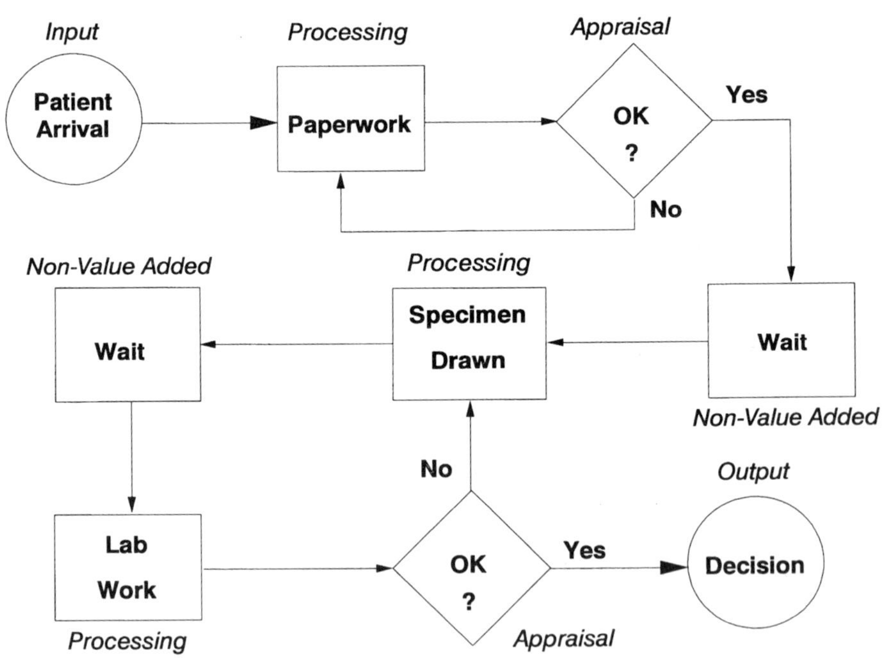

FIGURE 5.4 Patient Admissions Process

3. Wait.
4. Move to another location when notified.
5. Wait.
6. Be seen by nurse or physician for intervention.

Of these steps, only the last is of clinical value to the patient. From the hospital's perspective (see Figure 5.5), the patient is waiting but the hospital is consuming resources. The hospital believes—and acts as if—the consumption of these resources adds value to the patient because the consumption of the resources is an expense. The hospital pays for the admitting clerk, maintaining the building, the nurse and physician the patient will see, and all the other attending employees, whether the patient waits or not. The question is: Is the use of all those resources during the wait of the same value to this patient?

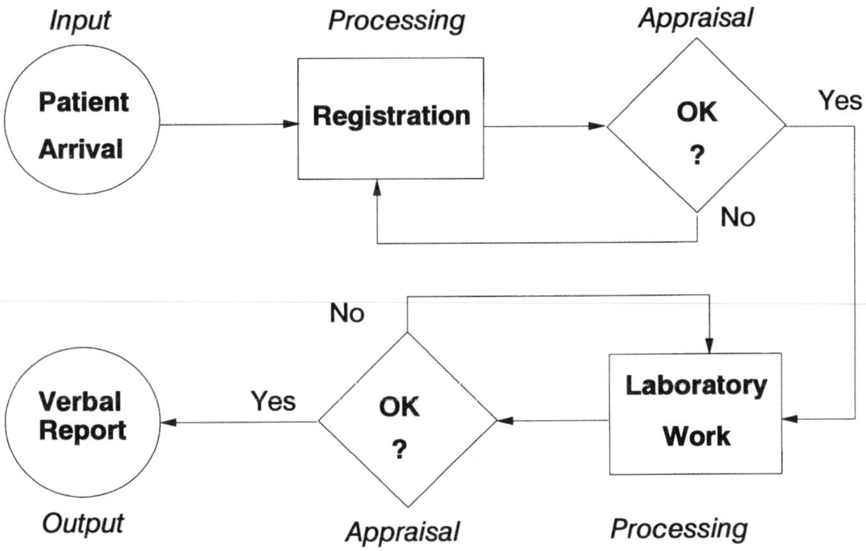

FIGURE 5.5 Patient Admissions Process from the Hospital's Perspective

With appropriate changes, the same type of question must be answered for EVA and BVA processes. This question leads to the recognition that outcome measures are a type of value-added measure and that there are three types of VA measures (see Table 5.1).

In contrast, processes can be non-value-adding. This means that the activities and associated resources are also NVA. Some examples of non-value-added processes, activities, and resources include:

- Excessive number of different employees visiting patient in a 24-hour period.
- Delayed response time to call lights.
- Waiting for intervention because of missing data (e.g., test results or a patient profile).
- Number of unnecessary forms required per order or patient.
- Number of minutes beyond one hour after antibiotic prophylaxis is given.
- Postponement of same-day surgery.
- Amount of expired inventory.

Another measure of PVA is the proportion of the budget spent on PVA resources. For example, you could list the major budget items (e.g., medical and technical, scheduling,

TABLE 5.1. Value-Added Measures

Business	Employee	Patient
• Financial	• Work environment	• Outcomes
• Operational	• Satisfaction	• Satisfaction

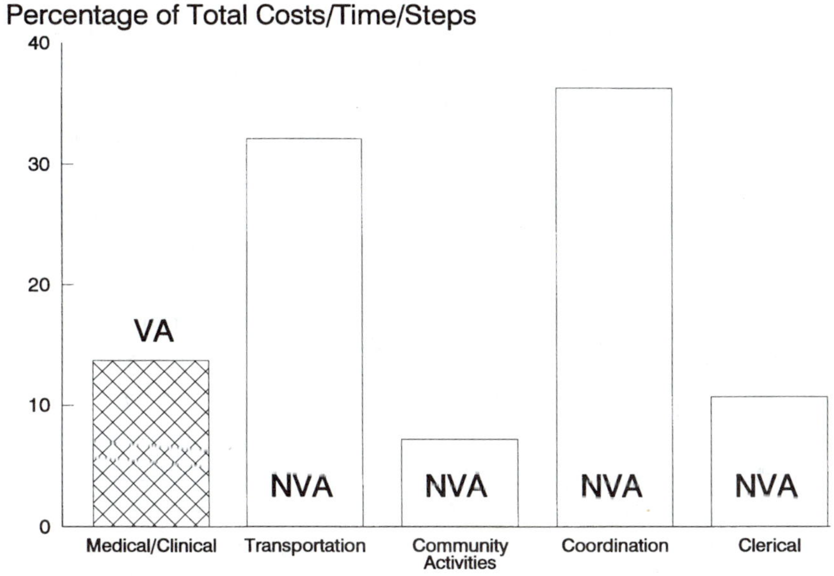

FIGURE 5.6 Budget Item Value

room and board, transportation, management, and documentation) and then determine which resources should add value to the patient (see Figure 5.6). In addition, patient satisfaction can also be used to measure PVA. For example, each item in Figure 5.6 may result in more or less patient satisfaction as the patient perceives the value of that activity, the length of time it takes to complete, and the disposition of the healthcare staff member during the activity.

CYCLE TIME

Value-added is time dependent. For example, hospital profit margins are around 4 percent. So, in one fiscal year, the total revenues are 1.04 times the total expenses. Suppose that same amounts of expenses were incurred during 12.5 months rather than 12 months. Or, if the revenues that typically are received in 12.5 months are now received in 12 months. The percent profit margin would double. How can the time to incur the expenses be increased or the time to receive the revenues be decreased? Simply by increasing productivity, which is the rate at which value is added to patients, employees, or the business. To put it another way, *productivity = value / time.*[2]

The purpose of value-added analysis is to identify those processes that are not efficient and to eliminate activities and their associated resources that are unnecessary. Resources are unnecessary if they delay service, do not contribute to the clinical outcome or patient satisfaction, or are redundant. While ABC is useful for getting more accurate cost information, VA analysis is useful for assessing the delivery of products and services. This requires understanding cycle time.

Cycle time for an organization is the total time from the moment the customer's need is identified to the time payment is received.[3] This is the total business cycle time. A healthcare organization can define the total healthcare cycle as the time the patient need is identified to the time payment is received. Unless the healthcare organization also includes the time to receive payment, much effort can be spent on improving PVA processes while jeopardizing the business because of poor EVA and BVA processes. Cycle time for processes is the time the input is received to the time the output is delivered. The patient cycle time is typically in hours or days, while the business cycle time is in weeks or months. Reducing the business cycle time means reducing accounts receivable average time, which would benefit the organization with increased cash flow.

Just as the executive in chapter 1 saw that budgets institutionalize losses by padding the expense accounts, processes institutionalize delays by padding the time account. Padding in time accounts is called lead time. The overall process of delivering an X-ray comprises several subprocesses: admis-

2. Stalk Jr., George and Hout, Thomas M. *Competing Against Time.* New York: The Free Press, 1990.

3. Meyer, Christopher. *Fast Cycle Time.* New York: The Free Press, 1993.

sions, instructions, setup, X-ray, and set-down. Because the owner of each process can no longer count on just-in-time delivery of the input it requires, the process integrates these subprocesses by padding them with lead times. The overall cycle times become inflated with the lead times (see Figure 5.7).

The sum of the actual cycle times for each subprocess is much shorter than the total process cycle time. This is why looking at the process with the largest scope to address cycle time efficiency is important. Each subprocess owner may reduce its cycle time without removing the lead times. However, it is still possible that within the subprocess, cycle time efficiency is low because of delays and poor design.

For example, the clinical process consists of such subprocesses as work-up, X-ray, diet, lab test, surgery, transfusion, postoperative care, discharge plan and instructions, medications (see Figure 5.8). Each of these subprocesses has its own cycle time from the moment the subprocess is triggered by a demand for its activities until the end of those activities. Some subprocesses can be triggered by the same de-

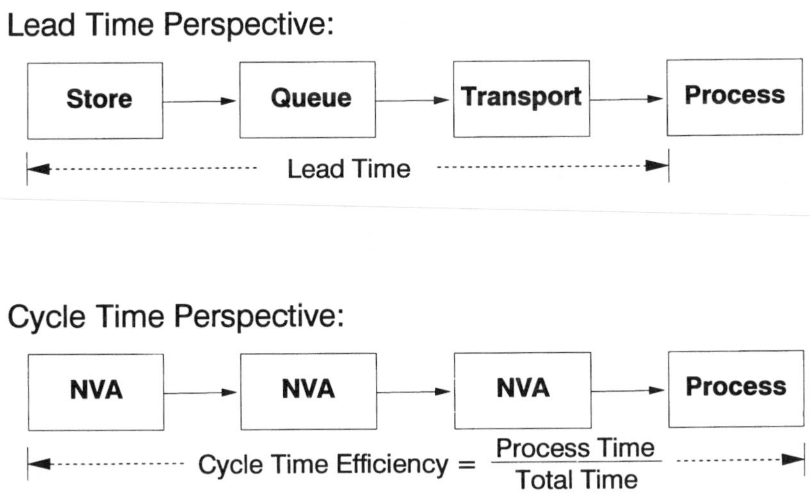

FIGURE 5.7 Lead Time and Cycle Time Perspectives

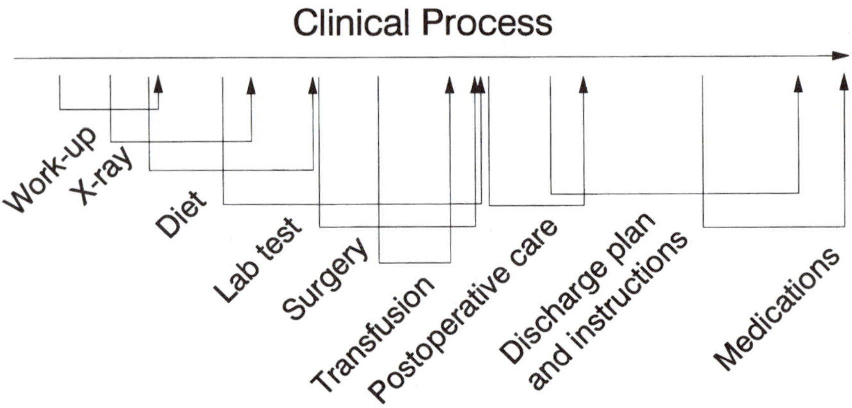

FIGURE 5.8 Clinical Process Subprocesses

mand and the activities can therefore be performed concurrently. Others must occur sequentially. Sequential subprocesses often cause delays, lead time, and NVA consumption of resources.

MEASURES OF VALUE-ADDED EFFICIENCY

As the executive in chapter 1 discovered, the profit-and-loss statement does not contain information in a readily available form needed to calculate the value-efficiency of an organization's efforts. Cycle time is an indication of the rate at which value is added. Cycle time efficiency is simply the ratio of the process time spent adding value to the total cycle time of the process. This ratio can also be multiplied by 100 to express it as a percent. Two value-efficiency measures are:[4]

- the ratio of costs associated with value-added resources to the total cost of all resources consumed

Cost-efficiency = Cost of VA/(Cost of VA and NVA)

4. Northey, Patrick and Southway, Nigel. *Cycle Time Management.* Portland, OR: Productivity Press, 1993.

- the ratio of time taken by all value-added activities to the total time taken by all activities

Time-efficiency = Time of VA/(Time of VA and NVA)

VA can also be measured directly as the number of VA steps the patient, employee, or business takes to the total number of steps. To increase cycle time efficiency, the number of NVA steps can be reduced.

Hospitals are prone to low cycle time efficiencies because of centralization of ancillary and support services. This requires patients and other things, such as, specimens, to be transported, and the staff to transport themselves, to various locations. Transportation adds no value to the clinical outcome, and by asking any patient, you know it does nothing for patient satisfaction.

For example, the cycle time for process for chemotherapy patients may be four days (see Figure 5.9): one day of bulking up on liquids, one day of treatment, two days of recuperation. The average patient yields a net profit to the hospital with this cycle time. Closer scrutiny reveals that some pa-

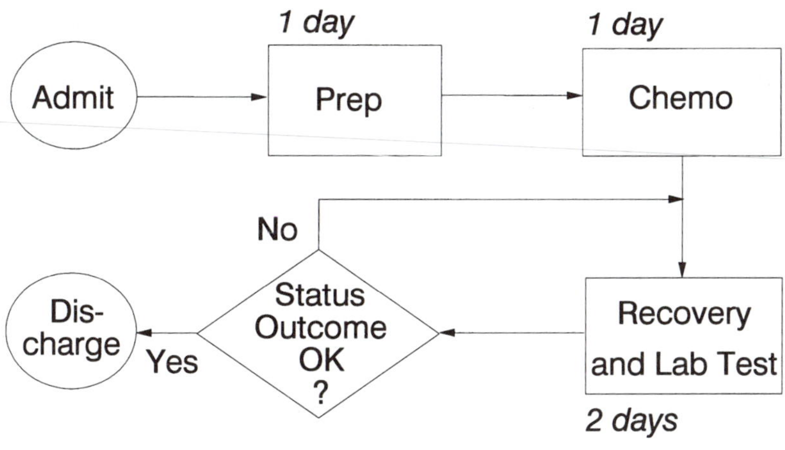

FIGURE 5.9 Cycle Time for Chemotherapy Patients

tients could leave after one day of recuperation if their negative blood test result was returned by 5:00 p.m. on the third day. However, the laboratory's policy is to postpone blood tests for all routine requests received after 2:00 p.m. until 7:00 a.m. the next morning.

The cycle time efficiency for the blood test for these patients was an average of 0.2 percent: a two-minute test (VA time) took 16 hours (VA + NVA time) from the time it was ordered until the time the result was picked up by the doctor and used to release the patient. The laboratory had optimized its processes by doing satellite testing in the afternoons (see Figure 5.10). This caused satisfied satellite customers but increased the length of stay for the chemotherapy patients by 25 percent, increased the hospital costs, and increased the charges to the patient.

In admissions, having efficiencies of less than 10 percent is not atypical. By following a patient from the moment he or

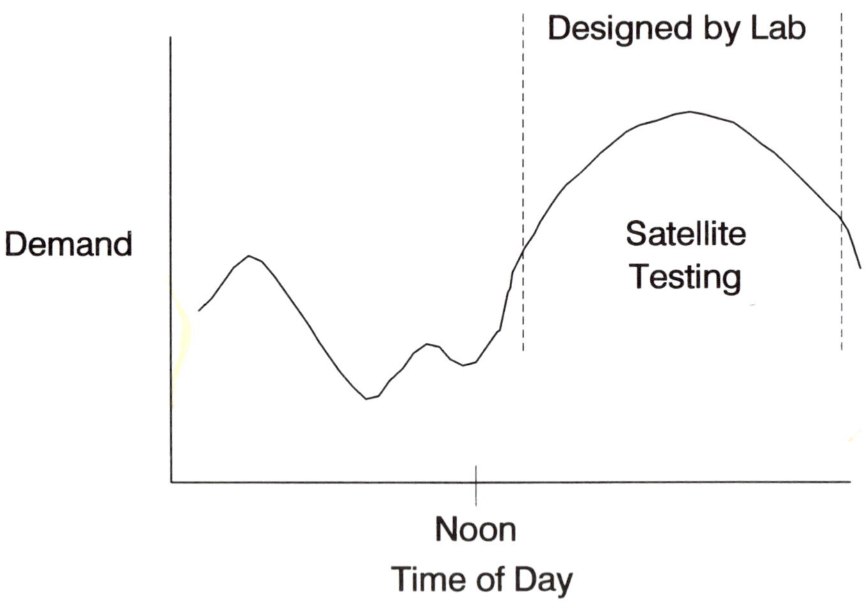

FIGURE 5.10 Lab Test Demand for Time of Day

she arrives until he or she leaves, you can collect data on cycle time efficiencies for various processes. A simple chart with columns for the steps the patient goes through and times for each step, are quite revealing. Such a chart connects quality, delivery, and costs (see Figure 5.11). The first column contains the steps or activities. The next three columns are data on value, cost, and time for those activities. This helps in identifying what activities add value, what their costs are, and how much time it takes to deliver the product or service. For example the patient from Figure 5.4 spent 187 minutes at the hospital, of which 11 minutes were value-added, for an efficiency of about 6 percent.

By extending the concept of critical pathways from only clinical information to include quality and delivery information, a more rigorous connection can be made between quality, delivery, and cost. For example, one hospital had an average length of stay of 3.8 days for AV graft thrombectomy. Medicare reimbursed for only one day. By tracking simultaneously the patient and delivery of healthcare services

#	Activity/Step	Value	Cost	Time (minutes)
1	Arrive at Admissions	NVA	Depends on how costs are assigned	4
2	Register	BVA		12
3	Wait	NVA		33
4	Move to Cashier	NVA		6
5	Arrange payment	BVA		7
6	Move to radiology	NVA		4
7	Wait	NVA		11
8	Go to dressing room	NVA		1
9	Change to smock	NVA		2
10	Wait	NVA		3
11	Move to X-ray room	NVA		1
12	X-ray	PVA		3
13	Return to dress	NVA		4
14	Change	NVA		2
15	Leave	NVA		5
Total				88

FIGURE 5.11 Sample Cycle Time Efficiency Data Chart

through the critical pathway with the times and expenses, this hospital could identify when the expenses exceeded the reimbursement. The task for the quality improvement team was then to reorganize the process to reduce the length of stay. One cause was identified as weekend stays for 63 percent of the patients due to lack of physical therapists or equipment. Reducing this to 4 percent reduced the length of stay to 2.5, with an immediate reduction in net loss to the hospital through improved cycle time efficiency and an improvement of the value-added rate.

In chapter 4, we saw that tracking the demand flow from cost objects to activities to resources required for those activities makes more accurate cost estimates possible. Using ABC will result in some change in the profitability of certain products and services (see Figure 5.12[a] and [b]). To improve

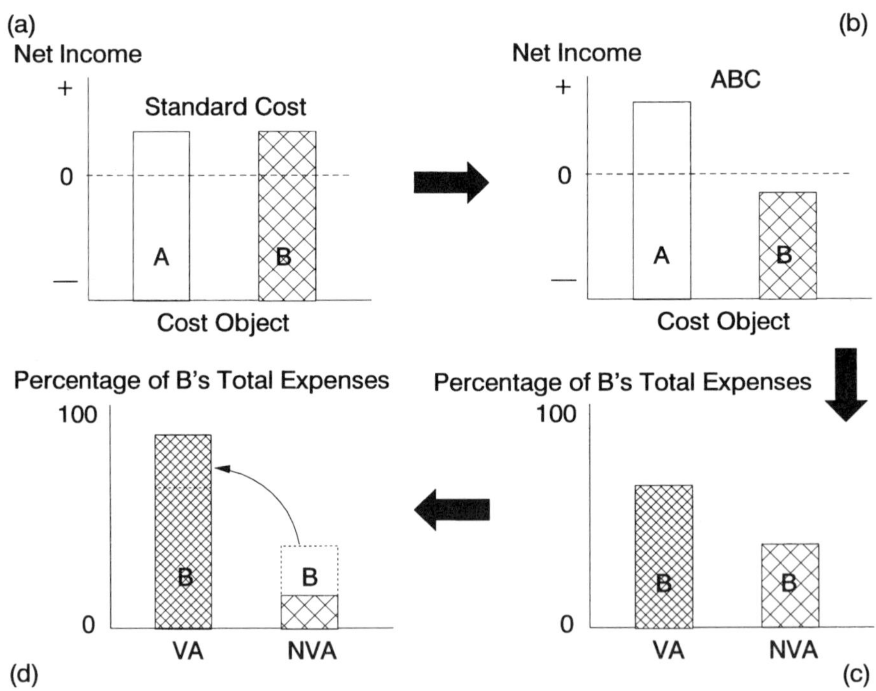

FIGURE 5.12 More Accurate Cost Estimates

the profitability of a product or service identified through ABC, do a value-added analysis first (see Figure 5.12c). By eliminating NVA activities or reducing their cost, the net profit can change. It may not change, however, if the resources are not reallocated to other VA activities (see Figure 5.12d).

Value-added analysis is useful for making immediate improvements to unprofitable service and product lines because it answers the question leading from the general ledger to the right-middle of Figure 2.4 "Which activities add value?" All NVA activities can and should be eliminated immediately, leaving only value-added activities.

6 The Cost of Quality

After processes are analyzed for the value they add, they can then be financially analyzed with respect to their quality level. ABC identifies more accurately the costs of processes (chapter 4); VA analysis identifies the delivery efficiency of those processes (chapter 5); and in this chapter we see how cost-of-quality (COQ) analysis identifies the quality of the value-added activities of processes. The uniqueness of COQ is that it converts quality into a financial measure so that the question "What does our quality cost?" can be answered. This allows the executive of chapter 1 to answer three questions:

1. What was the cost of poor quality and poor delivery of services to patients?
2. What was the cost of poor quality and poor delivery of services to employees?
3. What was the total cost for services to patients and employees?

COST OF QUALITY CATEGORIES

The sequence of activities that define a process are the actions of suppliers, processors, and customers. One key element in the definition of a process is the word "repeated." By repeating the sequence of activities of the process, you have an opportunity to improve by using the continuous improvement cycle (see Figure 3.1). The second time can be better than the first, the third better than the second, and so on. The first time you use a process you can determine its quality, delivery, and cost (Quality Delivery Cost or QDC) levels. This answers the question: What are the current quality, delivery, and cost levels of this process? Between the first and second time, you determine how it can be improved. This answers the question: How can these quality, delivery, and cost levels be improved? The second time you use the process it will yield new QDC levels. If these levels are better, the knowledge gained by finding answers to these two questions will have been successfully used to make improvements in the process.

For example, consider the process of the nurse administering medication. Each time this occurs it is a service unit. During a three-month period (see Figure 6.1), records showed that the average time spent not adding value was 17.53 minutes per service unit (delivery level), the average number of miss-

Activity	Time (minutes)
Searching	4.55
Calling	1.31
Redoing	6.02
Delivering	5.65
Total	17.53

Cost of drug = \$3.50 per dose; labor = \$23.50 per hour

Average number of missing doses per week = 84.6 (Quality)

Average cost per nonconformance = \$10.62 (Cost)

Average time spent per nonconformance = 17.53 minutes (Delivery)

FIGURE 6.1 Service Unit Records

ing doses per week was 84.6 (quality level), at a cost for the NVA activity and drugs of $10.62 per service unit (cost level).

After instituting some changes that included some cross-training of personnel, standardization of a medicine drop-off point, and establishment of a communications system to handle complaints, the new levels became: 8.63 minutes not adding value per service unit, 23.5 missing doses per week, and a cost of $7.13 per service unit. The annualized cost levels changed from $46,719.50 to $10,545.86, for a net savings of $36,173.64 for that year. The process has matured.

If evaluation of the process QDC reveals that the output does not conform to the patient needs or satisfy the patient, corrective action should be taken. Corrective action resolves a specific nonconformance of one output. For example, reoperating on a patient because of preventable, poor wound closure only corrects this nonconformance. This does not change the process, so it cannot improve the process. Preventive action improves subsequent results because the process is modified.

These types of process activities illustrate the basis for cost of quality categories:

- First you *design and develop* a process.
- Then you *use* the process.
- Third, you *evaluate* the process.
- Fourth, you *correct* any nonconforming result of the process.
- Finally, you may *redesign* the process to improve subsequent process results.

For existing processes, only the last four steps are used. These four steps identify the four cost-of-quality categories—[prevention, processing, appraisal, and failure.] These four steps are defined in Table 6.1. Examples and further clarification of these steps are described in the following sections.

TABLE 6.1. Cost-of-Quality Categories

Prevention	Costs to satisfy customer needs through redesign and development of systems and processes: the quality system.
Processing	Costs in using systems and processes to satisfy patients or customers: generation of conformance and nonconformance.
Appraisal	Costs to determine quality, delivery, and cost levels of systems and processes: degree of nonconformance.
Failure	Costs of the effect of and the activities and resources to correct system and process nonconformance.

Traditionally, failure costs are further classified as internal or external. Internal failure costs are those costs from failures found before the customer gets the output, while external failure costs are those costs from failures found after the customer gets the output. For example, a medication error discovered and corrected before the patient receives it may be classified as an internal failure, while correcting it afterward (no matter who discovered it) can be classified as an external failure. However, because these categories come from the manufacturing setting, they may not be as useful to healthcare organizations. In particular, for EVA and BVA processes, the identification of failures as internal and external makes less sense because the traditional cost-of-quality categories were initially not developed for EVA and BVA processes. Unless you can find a compelling reason for this further distinction, do not use it.

On the other hand, the addition of processing to the traditional list of COQ categories is useful. These four cost of quality categories match the four components of Shewhart and Deming's Plan-Do-Check-Act (PDCA) cycle: prevention costs can be viewed as planning costs; processing costs as doing costs; appraisal costs as checking costs; and failure costs as acting costs. Cost of quality adds to the PDCA cycle by distinguishing between preventive and corrective actions. Only the latter are viewed as acting.

PROCESSING COSTS

The process owner (or Processor in the SIPOC model) is responsible for three types of activities:

- Receiving quality input on time.
- Transforming the input to an output.
- Providing quality output on time.

The list of activities necessary to receive, transform, and deliver defines the process, for example:

- All medical services.
- All support services.
- All business services.
- Leadership.
- Management.

The costs of these activities are charged to the processing cost-of-quality category. Processing costs are necessary costs. Without them, there are no products or services (see Figure 6.2).

As wc saw in chapter 3, three types of processes are—BVA, EVA, and PVA—each with two classes of measures (see Table 5.1). This does not necessarily mean that there are, for example, two types of BVA processes, financial and operational. It does mean that a BVA process's outcome can be measured by its financial and operational effectiveness. To the extent these three types of processes are effective in meeting the needs of their respective customers, they add value.

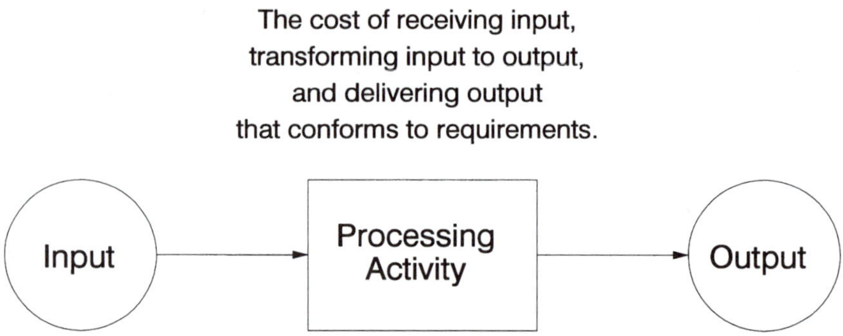

FIGURE 6.2 Processing Costs

PVA processes are processes related to direct medical, surgical, therapeutic, diagnostic care or intervention from nurses, physicians, physical therapists, and so on, for example:

- Urinalysis.
- Mastectomy.
- Coronary artery bypass graft.
- Administering medication.
- Radiation therapy.
- Immunization.

Any prevention, screening, diagnostic, therapeutic, or other management procedure to cure or ameliorate health problems or respond to healthcare needs, is a BVA process. Typically, these are the expenses associated with revenue centers.

These processes, however, must also personally satisfy patients, as indicated by patients, their families, and communities in patient-satisfaction surveys. Staff must therefore be courteous, have a positive attitude, and be respectful and considerate while they provide PVA services.

EVA processes are those that specifically contribute to working conditions (e.g., performance, compensation, recognition, development, safety, health, ergonomics, and employee-assistance programs). The value of these processes is measured by the degree to which they improve employee well-being and satisfaction as viewed by the employees.

BVA processes are designed to produce financial value to the organization. While PVA and EVA processes eventually do, other processes do so more directly. Some are activities directly aimed at generating capital (e.g., investments, capital acquisition, and philanthropy for nonprofit organizations). Others are aimed at the administrative, support, business, and operational side of the organization (e.g., billing, shipping, housekeeping, ancillary services, finance, materials management, patient transfer, payroll, insurance coding, records filing, scheduling, word processing, accounts receivable, and registration). These are the expenses associated with nonrevenue or cost centers.

Every process has three key characteristics:

1. Effectiveness.
2. Efficiency.
3. Adaptability.

Effectiveness refers to how well the process accomplishes its purpose (e.g., satisfying the patient, employee, or business needs). Efficiency refers to how well the process consumes resources in the transformation. Several measures of efficiency were identified in the previous chapter on VA analysis. Adaptability refers to the flexibility of the process to accommodate deviations and "special requests"—that is, how *efficient* the process is in *effectively* handling nonstandard requests.[1]

For example, the attending physician of a cancer patient undergoing repeated radiation treatment, requests a blood test

1. Harrington, H.J. *Business Process Improvement.* NY: McGraw-Hill, Inc., 1991, p. 180.

anywhere from 2:00 P.M. to 5:00 P.M. one day after the treatment. The testing system cannot process the two-minute test and doesn't report to the physician until the following morning. A negative result one day after the treatment would have allowed the patient to go home that day. When the clinical process is altered to allow the physician to order the test by 1:00 P.M. on the day after treatment to be able to release the patient, the test results are still not reported until the next day at 7:00 A.M.

When the laboratory gets the blood specimen, the medical technologist processes the test effectively in 12 minutes, consuming few resources of labor, capital, materials, and energy. The system, however, is not efficient: the cycle time exceeds 14 hours (5:00 P.M. to 7:00 A.M.), the cycle time efficiency for this part of the process is:

$$\frac{100\% \times 12 \text{ minutes}}{14 \text{ hours} \times \dfrac{60 \text{ minutes}}{1 \text{ hour}}} = 1.4\%$$

Even after the change, the special request is denied. The system is inflexible: it has not adapted to the change that could help both the patient and the hospital.

APPRAISAL COSTS

Appraisal costs are those costs associated with determining whether any organizational activity or use of resources conformed to expectations or requirements (see Figure 6.3). This is nothing more than the costs associated with answering the question: What are the current quality, delivery, and cost levels? The purpose of spending money on appraisals is to:

- Collect the necessary data and analyze it.
- Estimate quality, delivery, and cost levels.
- Provide data for establishing baselines for corrective and preventive action.

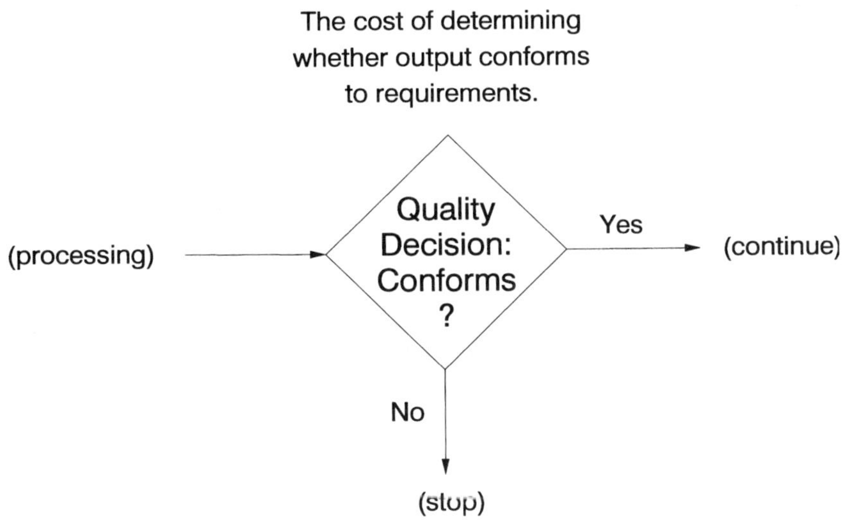

FIGURE 6.3 Appraisal Costs

- Create awareness and knowledge of quality, delivery, and costs of services.

In the medication process illustrated in Figure 6.1, the time spent to determine the quality, delivery, and cost levels is charged to the appraisal cost category. While appraisal costs do not add any value to the patient directly, they are necessary for continuous improvement. If this information, however, is never used to make those improvements, the appraisal costs would actually become NVA costs. Without this review of appraisal costs to see if they actually result in corrective or preventive action, estimates of total cost of quality categories will be misleading. This may mistakenly dissuade the organization not to use [the CICS concepts and tools] because there may not be adequate improvement as shown by the cost of quality analysis. Examples of activities that incur appraisal costs include:

- Inspection for accreditation, licensure, and certification.
- Resource utilization and chart reviews.

- Testing.
- Calibration material.
- Personnel qualification.
- Quality control.
- Accounting of cost data.
- Supplier certification and approval.
- Employee reviews and new-hire interviews.
- Medical staff credentialing.
- Audits.
- Patient surveys.

There are different types of appraisals, including 100 percent inspection, in-service inspection, acceptance sampling, statistical process control, and capability studies. The purpose of appraisals is to measure the effectiveness, efficiency, and adaptability of processes. Laboratories have numerous indices for measuring their efficiencies, including workload units and billable tests.

Physicians use a variety of tools that suggest ways to appraise clinical processes (e.g., practice parameters, critical paths, and outcome measures). Practice parameters or parameters of care define the critical interventions for appropriate care. For example, one parameter of care for asthmatics is the use of beta-agonists. The answer to "What is the purpose of this parameter of care?" suggests an appraisal measure for this clinical process. On the other hand, because critical paths *are* clinical processes or systematic approaches to medical decision making, which include standards, guidelines, and practice policies and options,[2] they are appraised by a variety of approaches (e.g., peer reviews and audits).

2. Office of Quality Assurance, American Medical Association. Attributes to guide the development of practice parameters. Chicago, IL: AMA, 1990.

FAILURE COSTS

Although processes are designed to be infallible, none are; failures *will* occur and they *will* cost. The goal must be to improve systems continuously, reducing fallibility. Failure costs are the costs associated with the nonconformance of process output to customer expectations (see Figure 6.4). Process failure costs are unnecessary costs for the patient, employee, and organization.

There are three reasons for spending money on failures, to:

1. Have a better understanding of the cause-effect relationships relevant to the failure.
2. Identify the critical few from the trivial many variables that influence a patient's dissatisfaction.
3. Provide clues (i.e., data, information, and profound knowledge) for corrective and preventive action.

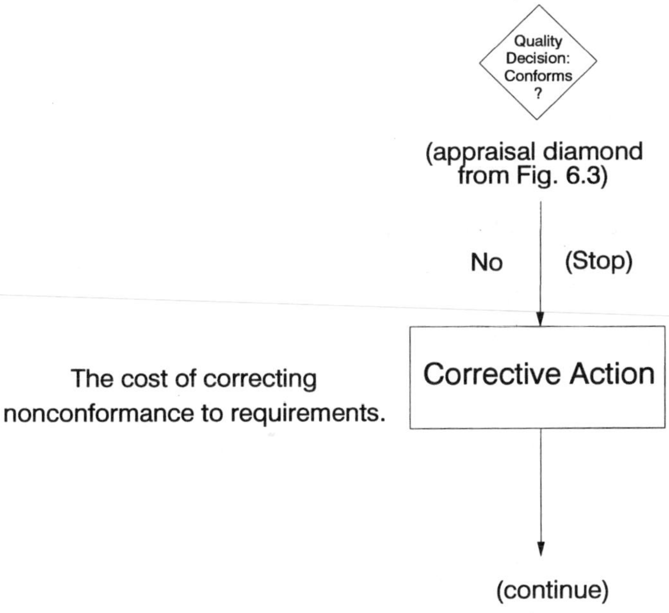

FIGURE 6.4 Failure Costs

For the medication process shown in Figure 6.1, the cost of the resources consumed to correct the missing medication incidents were failure costs. Additional failure costs were not calculated, including unproductive waits by other employees needing the nursing staff and others involved in the corrective action and any actual adverse clinical results due to the delays. These are corrective action costs because they only correct each failure as it occurs. Operational failure costs include:

- Time spent addressing patient complaints.
- Insurance billing errors.
- Inadequate number of personnel in anesthesiology.
- Inefficient OR scheduling.
- Lost specimens and results.
- Warranty claims.
- Backlogs.
- Misplaced patients.
- Schedules not met.
- Excessive overtime.
- Delayed and uncollected accounts receivables.
- Lack of compliance with regulations.
- Excessive turnover.
- Rework and scrap.
- Delays in new-service development cycle.
- Inaccurate or missing charts.
- Cross-functional priority conflicts.
- Lack of repeat patients.

Clinical failure costs include:

- Excessive or unnecessary hospital stays.
- Lack of follow-up.
- Unnecessary and inaccurate testing.
- Poor clinical outcomes.
- Medical and prescriptive errors.
- Prescribing adversely interactive medications.
- Coronary artery bypass graft for mild blockage of coronary arteries.
- Inaccurate or no measurement of fetus's head.

PREVENTION COSTS

Prevention costs can mean two things in healthcare. They may mean preventive medicine: that is, to increase or maintain a certain quality of life or add to a person's life expectancy. Whether this is achievable and measurable is an unresolved issue. However, prevention may also have another meaning: freedom from deficiencies or nonconformance in existing processes. Prevention costs are those costs that result in reduced nonconformance. An ideal way to test whether an activity is preventive is to eliminate it and see whether failures or nonconformances increase. If they do (when other factors are controlled), the activity is preventive. In healthcare, this approach may not always be ethical, so more planning may be required to identify potential causes and analyze them theoretically from an expert's perspective.

The key distinction between corrective action as a failure cost and preventive action as a prevention cost is that corrective action does not result in a change in the process—the failures or defects identified are merely corrected. Preventive action, however, does require a change in the process. Preventive action means correcting the process so that future defects will not occur.

Prevention costs are those costs associated with the initial design and development of a process or with subsequent redesigns and developments that lead to improved process performance, including:

- Quality planning.
- Development of measures.
- Education and training.
- Quality assurance.
- Maintenance.
- Equipment calibration.
- Design and development of services, systems, and processes.

For existing services, this means modifying the process (see Figure 6.5). Another way of looking at prevention costs is

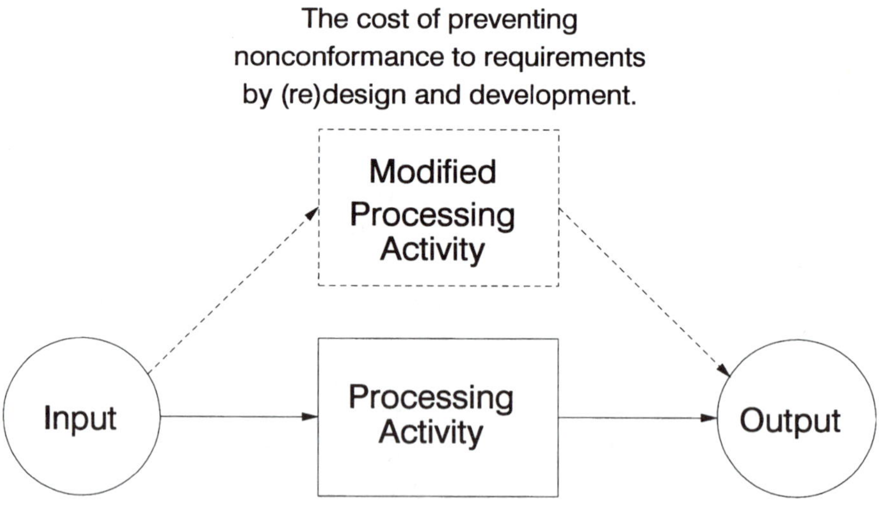

FIGURE 6.5 Prevention Costs

as the costs of those actions taken to plan and develop the process to ensure that there are no defects. Thus, the costs of redesigning existing processes to reduce or eliminate NVA and failure activities are considered prevention costs.

For the medication process in Figure 6.1, the cost of cross-training, designing, and developing the fax communications system and its communication form and standardization of the drop-off point are all charged to prevention costs. These are prevention costs and not corrective action costs because they alter the process, resulting in changes in future levels of quality, delivery, and cost.

Prevention costs are necessary for the organization's long-term survival. The purpose of spending money on prevention is to:

- Have a better understanding of the cause-effect relationships relevant to the imperfection in the process.
- Identify the critical few from the trivial many variables that influence the process.
- Provide clues (i.e., data, information, and knowledge) for processing activities.

When they lead to a change in the process, the following items are considered prevention costs:

- Quality planning.
- Data analysis.
- Development of measures or indicators.
- Controls for instruments and equipment.
- Preventive maintenance.
- Training.
- Supplier certification.
- Some QA/QC department expenses.
- Design reviews.

- Statistical process control.
- Prototypes.
- Standard operating procedures.
- Documentation.
- Preventive problem-solving.

Prevention costs can also include the cost associated with quality improvement teams. They do not include them if the teams are reacting to problems. Teams assigned to solve failures are corrective action teams. The training, resources, time, and cost of these teams' solutions are failure costs. The cost of quality improvement teams can be charged to prevention only when they are proactive—that is, when they are assigned the task of improving a process, not removing a patient's dissatisfaction.

For example, outpatient studies, which are considered an appraisal cost, reveal that 73 percent of the activities engaged by the staff to process a patient involve paperwork. A major source of this paperwork is unidentifiable sheets. The process is modified through redesign and development of several steps:

- Color-coded folders.
- Standardized memos and instructions for patients.
- In-service training of nurses.
- In-service training of clerical staff on units.
- Development, writing, and issuance of new policies and procedures in administration and preop.
- New forms.

The costs of designing and developing these modifications to the existing process are prevention costs.

TOTAL QUALITY COSTS

Traditionally, the costs associated with prevention, appraisal, and failure (internal and external) are called the costs of quality, or more exact, the costs of *poor* quality.[3] The idea behind this is that if processes were perfect, the costs of poor quality would be the costs that would disappear: there would be no need to prevent or appraise because there would be no failures. Thus, prevention and appraisal costs are those costs that exist because poor quality can exist, while failure costs are those costs that exist because failures do exist.[4] For example, the cost of sterilization of equipment is a prevention cost because infections *can* occur. The cost of medical audits is an appraisal cost because mistreatment *can* occur. Reoperations cost is a failure cost because failures *did* occur.

The cost of no failure is defined as the processing cost. It is the cost of using the process as designed because it is designed to achieve no failures. By adding it to quality costs, we have the total cost of quality (see Figure 6.6).

Figure 6.6 shows that quality is clearly not free but requires an investment—that is, the cost of designing and using the process. These are the costs of prevention and processing. A profit is made when the revenues generated from the selling of the output of the process exceed the total costs. If the cost of successfully redesigning (i.e., prevention) is less than the cost of failure and appraisal, the prevention cost has been a worthwhile investment.

Prevention and appraisal costs are sometimes called controllable costs of poor quality. If we were certain there would be no defects, these costs would not be needed. We control these costs by deciding whether to answer the ques-

3. Campanella, J. (Chair, Quality Costs Committee). *Guide for Reducing Quality Costs.* Milwaukee: ASQC, 1987. See also, Harrington.

4. Morse, Wayne J.; Roth, Harold P.; and Poston, Kay M. *Measuring, Planning, and Controlling Quality Costs.* Montvale, NJ: NAA, 1987.

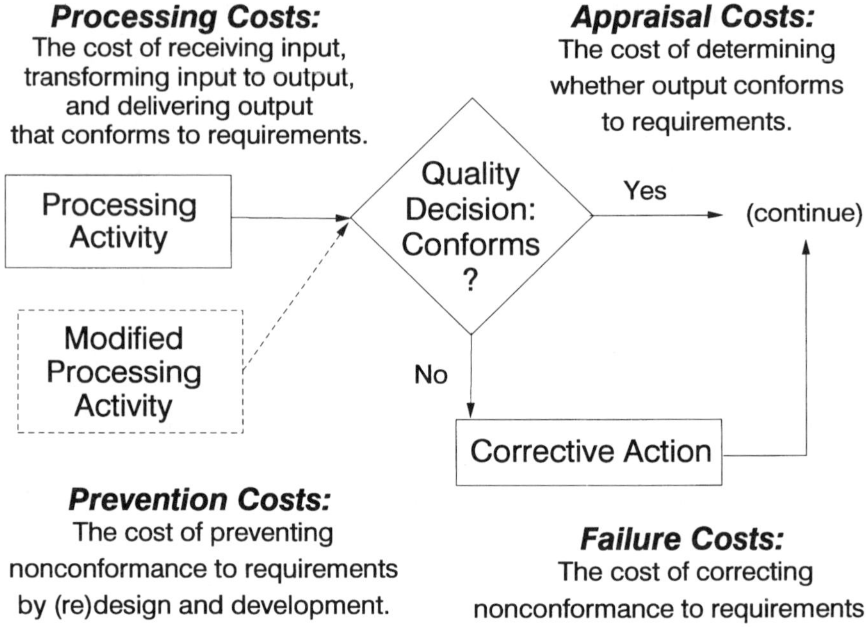

FIGURE 6.6 Total Cost of Quality

tions:What are the current quality, delivery, and cost levels? and How can these levels be improved? and take action on the answers we get. Failure costs are sometimes called resultant costs because they occur because of the fallibility of processes. Ignoring these costs does not make them disappear.

As the executive of chapter 1 discovered, hiding these costs among other costs also does not make them disappear. Instead, they pad the budget, making it difficult to identify where the opportunities are for reducing costs by improving quality and delivery. Figure 6.7 shows how traditional accounting views costs: all costs, no matter whether they add value or not or are used for correcting or preventing defects, are processing costs. By adding another level of detail, the costs can be assigned to processing, appraisal, failure, or prevention, as shown in Figure 6.8. Now it is clearer where the opportunities are.

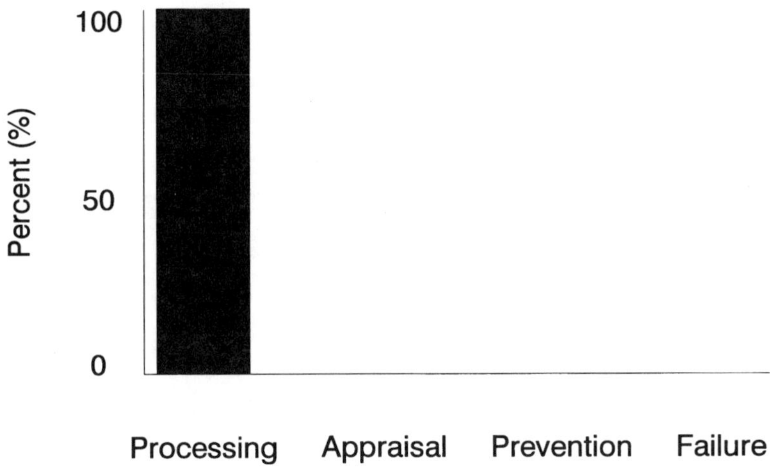

FIGURE 6.7 Traditional Accounting View of Costs

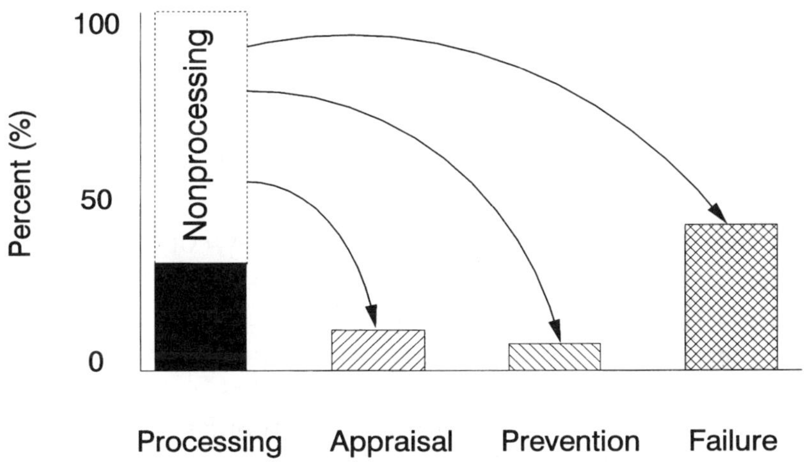

FIGURE 6.8 New, More Detailed View of Costs

The traditional view of cost of quality was that some optimal point existed at which reducing the number of failures was not worthwhile because the cost to do so exceeded the savings (see Figure 6.9). At this optimal point, the cost of *poor* quality—the sum of the costs for prevention, failure, and appraisal—was a minimum at some level of defects greater than

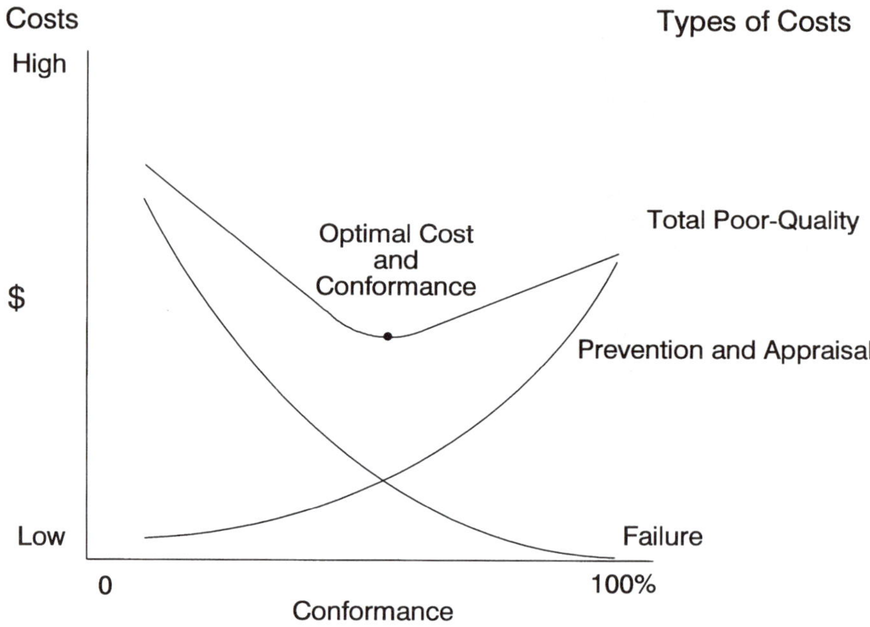

FIGURE 6.9 Traditional View of Cost of Quality

0 percent. This perspective is based on the nonquality assumption that profits can only be made by controlling costs. Direct costs were either controllable (prevention and appraisal) or a result of poor control (internal and external failure). The old view looks at processes as if they are all business-value-added processes.

However, the total quality management perspective recognizes that there are three major types of processes: customer (or patient)-value-added, employee-value-added, and business-value-added. The TQM perspective is that profits result from improving quality. The consequence of not recognizing these distinctions is not recognizing that there are other indirect costs in addition to the four cost of quality categories: costs incurred by customers, the cost of customer dissatisfaction, and the cost of poor reputation.[5] These additional costs also do not show up in the profit-and-loss

5. Harrington, H.J. *Poor-Quality Costs.* New York: Marcel Dekker, Inc., 1987.

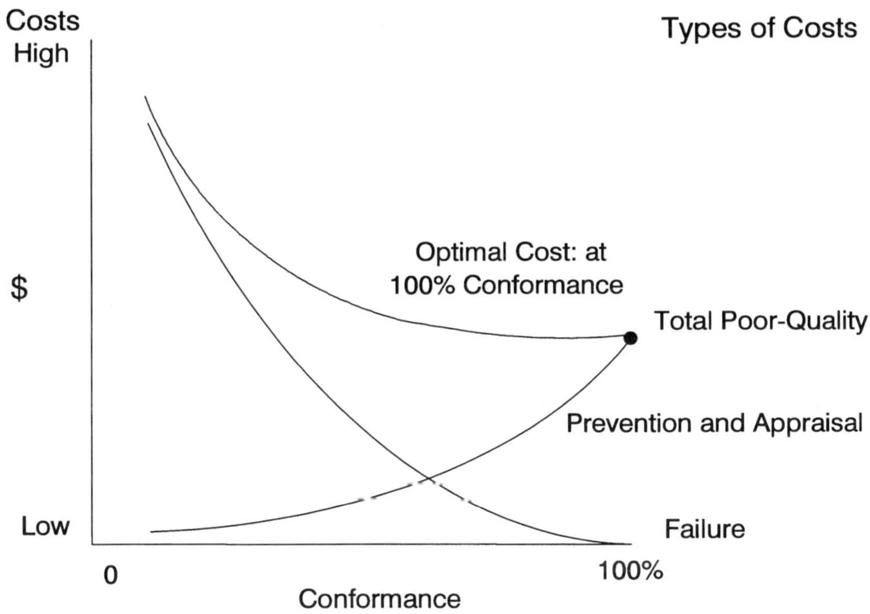

FIGURE 6.10 TQM View of Cost of Quality

statement and are difficult to estimate. However, they influence the business through decreased profits, implying that the optimal point is at 100 percent conformance (see Figure 6.10).[6] The new view, in line with continuous improvement, says that there are ways of redesigning processes so that they are less than the total costs of *poor* quality. That is, there is no point at which continuous improvement is no longer viable.

PROCEDURES FOR USING COST OF QUALITY CATEGORIES

The primary objective of a cost of quality system is to identify high-priority areas of wasted or nonconformance-producing

6. Atkinson Jr., John H.; Hohmer, Gregory; Mundt, Barry; Troxel, Richard B.; and Whichell, William. *Current Trends in Cost of Quality: Linking the Cost of Quality and Continuous Improvement.* Montvale, NJ: National Association of Accountants, 1991.

costs. Communication between the customer, processor, and supplier about the output forms a continuous improvement loop. Feedback, measurement, and evaluation are essential to continuous improvement. Using the quality improvement tools while following a cost-of-quality procedure should lead to improvements in the income statement that are attributable to improved patient satisfaction and clinical outcomes. Procedures are useful for implementing the cost-of-quality system in these five areas:

1. Process activity identification.
2. Appraisals.
3. Corrective actions.
4. Preventive actions.
5. Continuous improvement.

The following sections examine the procedures for the first four areas. Chapter 7 discusses continuous improvement.

Processing activities yield a level of quality, delivery, and cost for a fixed amount of repetitions. For example, all the patients during the last three months with a specific DRG provide the basis for estimating the quality, delivery, and costs of the processes associated with that DRG. Appraisal activities are used to collect and analyze the appropriate data. Failure activities are used to address nonconformance, and prevention activities are used to reduce the number of nonconformances or dissatisfactions (i.e., quality), the length of stay (i.e., delivery), and the amount billed (i.e., cost).

Procedures for identifying processing activities

The key to successful use of cost-of-quality categories is in identifying which activities belong to which categories. The definitions given in Table 6.1 are general statements about each category. Each organization must develop its own specific definitions so that activities and resources can be assigned to the categories. Most activities are readily identifiable. Many, however appear to be more than one type of cost. The objective is to classify activities as accurately as possible. It is not to define every movement. Costs are estimated, so some amount of inaccuracy can be expected.

For example, from the general definition of failure costs, the organization would define subcategories related to specific aspects of delivering healthcare services from vendors to design to delivery, for example:

- Supplier or purchasing failures.
- Marketing failures.
- Design of new products and services failures.
- Administrative failures.
- Delivery of services failures.

In each of these areas, there are specific elements to the failure costs. These could be defined by each department, function, or revenue center. For example, failures in delivery of healthcare services may be due to a failure of:

- The purchasing department to order the right amount of, for example, syringes.
- The laboratory to turn around a result in two hours.
- The surgeon to follow protocol.
- The housekeeping staff to prepare a bed within one hour of admission.

You will also need a procedure for identifying which activities and resources belong to either the three value-added categories (i.e., patient, employee, and business) or the non-value-added (NVA) category. This is the key to accurate assignment of resources and activities. Then, through activity-based costing, the activities and resources triggered by the appropriate cost objects (i.e., patients, employees, and business) are assigned to these categories also.

Procedures for appraisals

There are five objectives of an appraisal process:

1. It must provide reliable cost-effective estimates of quality, delivery, and costs.
2. It must be used to assess critical processes, products, and services, and their critical characteristics.
3. Its data must be easily recorded, documented, retrievable, and accessible.
4. It must provide useful information for corrective and preventive action.
5. It must be reviewed for continuous improvement.

For example, a medical audit is used to appraise clinical procedures. Steps to ensure that the medical audit complies with the criteria for useful appraisals would include:

- Developing objectives for reducing costs by improving the quality and delivery of clinical procedures.
- Developing audit procedures and criteria for quality, delivery, and cost.
- Identifying procedures that are high-risk, high-volume, and problem-prone.
- Analyzing variations in quality, delivery, and costs.
- Evaluating the return on the cost of the medical audit.

The simplest kind of appraisal is a 100 percent inspection. However, the information from any inspection must be used to improve. This requires that you continue around the continuous improvement cycle to answer the question: How can quality, delivery, and cost levels be improved? The appraisal process must feed data to procedures for corrective actions and for preventive actions for each component of the organizational system: the business, suppliers, patients or customers, and employees.

The appraisal process is the first step to an approach for using "data related to quality, customers, clients, constituents, and operational performance, with relevant financial data . . . to support organizational-level review, action, and planning."[7] If appraisal data do not lead to action, the appraisal process is wasteful. There are two kinds of actions that should be triggered by appraisals (see Table 6.2):

1. Immediate corrective action on problems found.
2. Longer-term preventive action to improve processes.

Procedures for corrective actions

A procedure for becoming aware of and addressing failures to satisfy patients or customers and be competitive should:

- Use measures of patient satisfaction.
- Use measures of patient dissatisfaction.
- Generate data on failures, successes, responsiveness, problem solving, and their costs.
- Use a problem-solving procedure for corrective actions.

---

7. 1995 Malcolm Baldrige National Quality Award Criteria. NIST, Route 270 and Quince Orchard Road, Administration Building, Room A537, Gaithersburg, MD 20899-0001.

TABLE 6.2. Appraisal Data

PURPOSE	INTERNAL OPERATIONS	SUPPLIERS	PATIENTS OR CUSTOMERS	EMPLOYEES
To develop priorities for prompt solutions to problems.	Increase organizational satisfaction through corrective action.	Increase supplier satisfaction through corrective action.	Increase patient or customer satisfaction through corrective action.	Increase employee satisfaction through corrective action.
To determine key trends and correlations to support status review, decision making, and longer-term planning.	Increase organizational satisfaction through preventive action.	Increase supplier satisfaction through preventive action.	Increase patient or customer satisfaction through preventive action.	Increase employee satisfaction through preventive action.

Without awareness of failures, it is impossible to make corrections, much less improvements. Measures are a necessary part of becoming aware. Patients usually have a different opinion of your quality than you do. You need to be aware of patient satisfaction, so that you continue to do those things that satisfy patients. You also need to be aware of patient dissatisfaction, so you can correct and improve. The following questions may help you in creating awareness and in developing your corrective action procedure:

- How is patient dissatisfaction and satisfaction determined?
- How do you handle patient dissatisfaction and satisfaction?
- How do you know whether failures occur and how often they do?
- How is failure data recorded?
- Are failure costs documented?
- Who records and documents failures?
- How accessible or retrievable are the data?
- How are you and others trained to solicit comments from patients and your customers, anticipate problems, handle problems, and listen to patients and your customers?
- Are data analyzed by patient groups or segments and for trends?

Procedures for preventive actions

The primary purpose of prevention is to reduce failure costs. A secondary purpose is to reduce the other quality costs: appraisal, processing, and prevention. Prevention costs are good costs because they go toward reducing failures (i.e., improving quality) and reducing total costs. They will only be effective in achieving these goals if knowledge about your processes is accurate.

To get the most leverage from your prevention costs, start as far upstream in the process as possible to first identify failures and then ways to reduce the other quality costs. The earlier on in the process a failure occurs, the more non-value is added to the service as it is processed. In the end, however, because of the failure, the total cost may be lost if the service is repeated or rejected. If the failure can be corrected, failure costs are added. This results in a lower profit for the organization or, if it is passed on to the patient, a lower perceived-value by the market.

A prevention procedure should have these characteristics:

- It addresses every aspect of the business (i.e., every phase of the service and product development and delivery cycle) from design of services and products to marketing and sales to follow up.
- It is a regular and integral part of the business or your job.
- It is proactive.
- It receives information from the appraisal and failure (corrective action) procedures.
- Its leverage is maximized by starting with critical processes and as far upstream as possible.
- It includes a problem-solving procedure.
- It is data-based.
- It has a continuous improvement loop to evaluate its effectiveness and its return on investment.

APPLYING COST OF QUALITY

For example, a patient is admitted for gastrointestinal elective surgery. Two days after surgery it is discovered that the

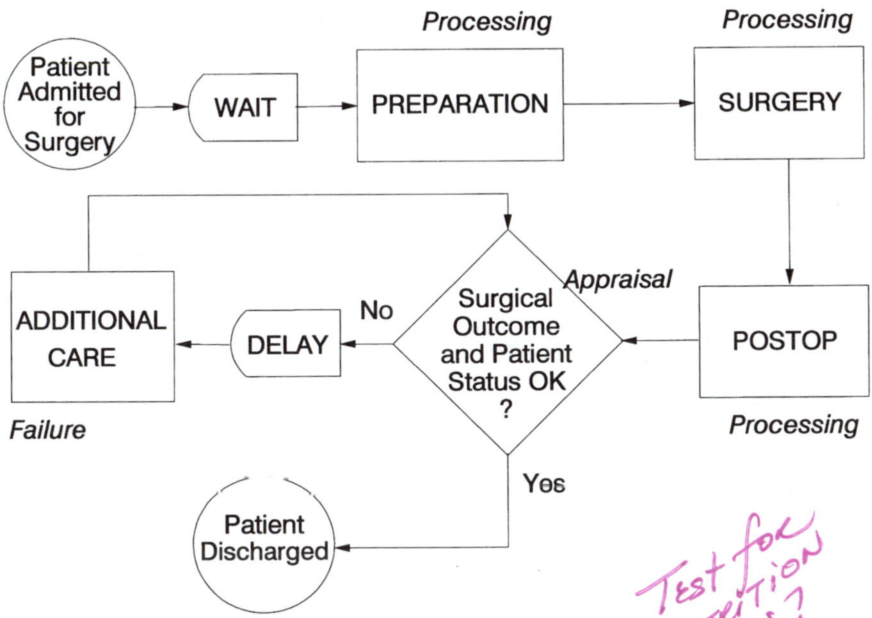

FIGURE 6.11 General Steps for Sample Patient

patient suffers from protein-calorie malnutrition (PCM), an affliction affecting as many as 50 percent of hospitalized patients.[8] The general steps this patient took and the cost-of-quality category to which each step belongs are illustrated in Figure 6.11.

One estimate of the costs of each of these categories is shown in Figure 6.12. For a particular patient, it appears that the failure cost is twice the cost of processing. The costs defined as preventive costs are preventive for the kinds of failures that may arise from the surgical activities. They may now be included as part of processing. There are no prevention costs to prevent malnutrition in a patient whose primary

8. Reilly, J.J.; Hull, S.F.; Albert, N.; et. al. "Economic impact of malnutrition: A model system for hospitalized patients," *JPEN* 1988;12:371. Also, Meguid, M.M.; Mughal, M.M.; Meguid, V. "Risk-benefit analysis of malnutrition and perioperative nutritional support; A review." *Nutrition International* 1987; 3:25–34.

Activity	Costs	Category
PREOP Bowel prep, prophylactic, antibiotics, anesthesia	$ 134	Prevention/ Processing
SURGERY Team, procedure resources	$ 1,491	Processing
POSTOP Patient care unit resources	$ 5,867	Processing
DISCHARGE Ambulatory, eating	$ 68	Appraisal
ADDITIONAL CARE ***Feeding TPN, antibiotics, reoperation, ICU and non-ICU care***	***$14,352***	***Failure***

FIGURE 6.12 Costs and COQ Categories of Sample Patient Activities

diagnosis is GI elective surgery. The appraisal cost is low because it is after-the-fact. However, the failure costs are high because of this. Corrective action resolves the matter with this one patient. The process is not modified to prevent other similar patients from undergoing the same failure.

You can answer the executive's questions about how to reduce costs by improving quality and delivery using the cost of quality categories and their procedures. The answers to these questions complete the analysis of general ledger items by providing three additional levels of detail to the traditional financial information (see Figure 2.5).

For example, some nonnursing costs are types of expense that could benefit from activity-based costing by allocating them to particular patients—the wide, horizontal arrow in Figure 6.13—rather than using standard costs based on an average of all nonnursing costs (see Figure 4.1). This would provide more accurate information about the nonnursing cost for patient

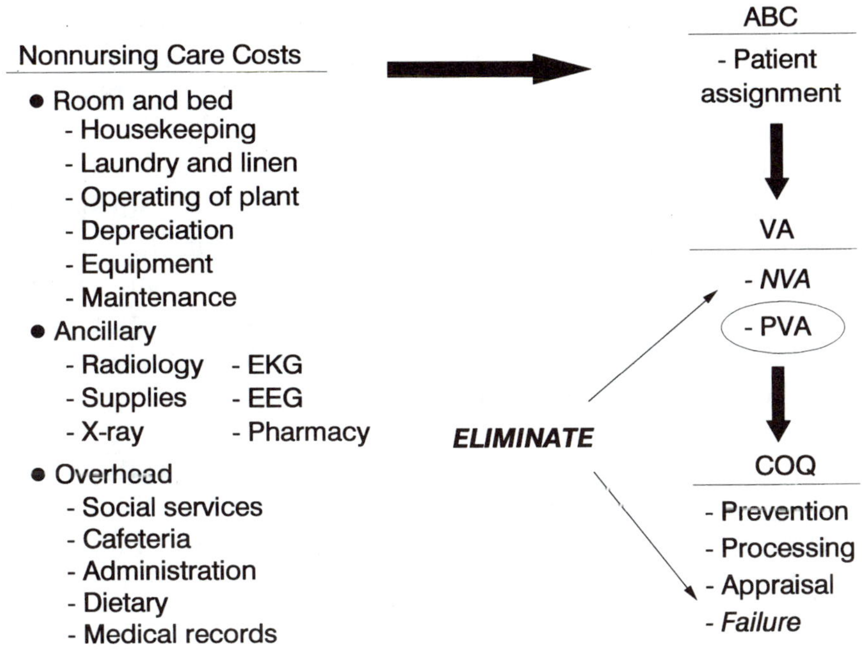

FIGURE 6.13 Cost Allocating Using . . .

types (e.g., DRG-acuity level). You would be better informed about the profitability of your services and product lines.

Value-added analysis would help identify those steps and resources consumed without adding value to the patient, either clinically or operationally—the top, vertical arrow in Figure 6.11. Elimination of NVA activities and reallocating them to VA activities would have an immediate impact on the bottom line. Finally, the remaining VA activities can be further classified according to their COQ category—the second vertical arrow in Figure 6.13. This allows further improvement of the bottom line by reducing the failure costs.

OVERVIEW

Chapters 4 through 6 contain descriptions of the concepts and tools comprising the analyses described in Figure 2.4.

These analyses take general ledger items and view them in three different ways to extract more useful information for effecting reductions in cost by improving quality and delivery of healthcare services. This has been accomplished by recognizing that traditional financial and accounting information answers some questions about costs and profits, but not all. In today's competitive environment, where quality, access, and patient satisfaction are driving healthcare organizations, new questions are raised that cannot be answered by the traditional approach to finance and accounting. New approaches are needed—namely, activity-based costing, value-added analysis, and cost of quality.

The remaining chapters are dedicated to illustrating how these concepts and tools can be used to reduce the cost of quality and delivery and how to develop these analyses to supplement the traditional, and still necessary, financial and accounting analyses.

7 The Continuous Improvement Cycle System

The key to a successful quality initiative is the ability to incorporate continuous improvement thinking into the organization. New knowledge and new skills are constantly required to cope with an ever-changing competitive environment, which is due to changing customer needs and new technology. Organizations that do not change are passed by. Organizations, however, can only change because their employees are changing. If your organization is not making improvements as part of that change, it will be passed by other organizations that are.

With the concepts of the previous four chapters, the senior executive of chapter 1 can identify five skills required for continuous improvement:

1. The ability to analyze quality and delivery as costs.
2. The ability to understand process variation.
3. The ability to learn and acquire new knowledge.
4. The ability to solve problems based on that new knowledge.
5. The ability to manage cycle-time.

The framework for integrating these skills, called the continuous improvement cycle system (CICS), is shown in Figure 7.1.

To answer the question What are the current quality, delivery, and cost levels (Q1)? you must incur an appraisal cost. The information gained is factual information about the lev-

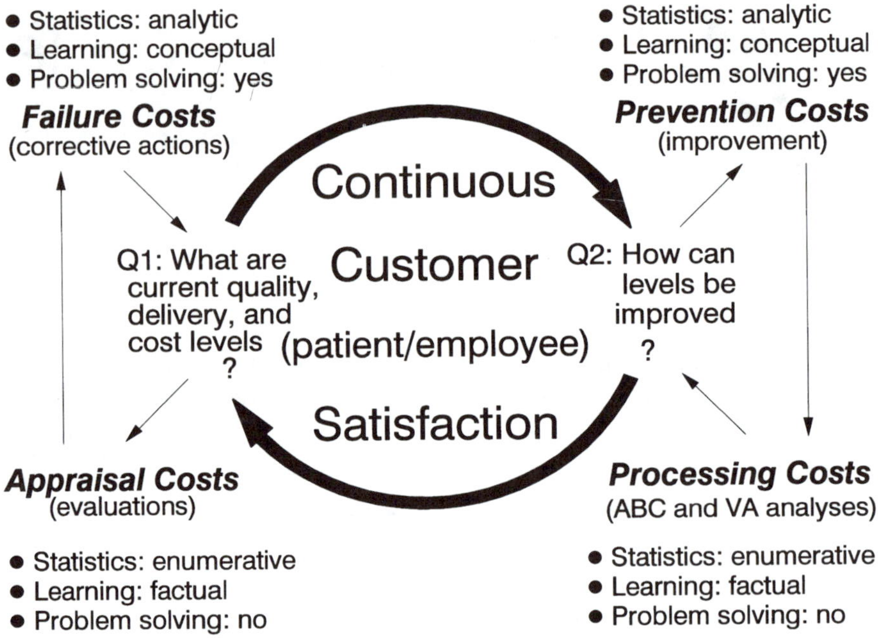

FIGURE 7.1 The Continuous Improvement Cycle System

els of quality, delivery, and cost. It may come from a review of charts, resource utilization, outstanding receivables, denial of claims, employee suggestions, or from patient complaints and feedback. When a nonconformance is discovered, corrective action is taken. This incurs failure costs. To solve the nonconformance will often require problem solving, which requires more than factual information. It requires conceptual knowledge about that particular incident.

Sometimes we don't get that knowledge and we ignore the failures. Other times we attempt to rectify the dissatisfaction but do nothing about the process. It stays the same. If we use the same process under the same conditions, we shouldn't be surprised to get the same results. Too often we continue in this way.

Instead, we could take the information we get from the appraisal and start redesigning the process to make it better by reducing the rate of nonconformances. This will incur a prevention cost. We could answer the question: How can the current levels of quality, delivery, and cost be improved (Q2)? This will also require problem solving and learning conceptually about the process.

Once we have the process modified, we can start using it again. This new process will have its own set of activities that add value and those that do not, though the proportions will differ from the previous design. The new process should not only better satisfy the patient needs, but also be more cost-effective and increase employee well-being. The appropriate data can help ensure that it will, but you will need to determine the new quality, delivery, and cost levels. You return to Q1 and incur additional appraisal costs.

COST-OF-QUALITY AND DELIVERY SKILLS

The skills needed to analyze quality and delivery as costs include the ability to:

- Estimate costs accurately enough for the types of decisions to be made using activity-based drivers.
- Determine whether resource consumption adds value and for whom.
- Estimate the cost of poor quality.

The difference between traditional cost accounting and cost-of-quality accounting is in the type and amount of information they provide. Traditional cost accounting operates under the equation:

$$\text{Net Profit} = \text{Revenues} - \text{Expenses}$$

This leads to identifying different types of expenses (e.g., salaries, fees, and depreciation). Then each type of expense is analyzed by how it accumulates. Salaries, for example, accumulate by number of people, wage levels, projects and services, departments, units, and organization. An analysis of salaries by this method would result in a single bar if the result were depicted graphically (see Figure 7.2a). This analysis makes three assumptions:

1. Processes do not vary in their consumption of resources.
2. An equivalent amount of resource always provides the same value.
3. Each dollar spent on the same type of resource is used the same way.

Traditional cost analyses depend on the accuracy of the estimates of the separate costs. Activity-based costing does not assume that processes do not vary in their consumption of resources. It can therefore provide better estimates because

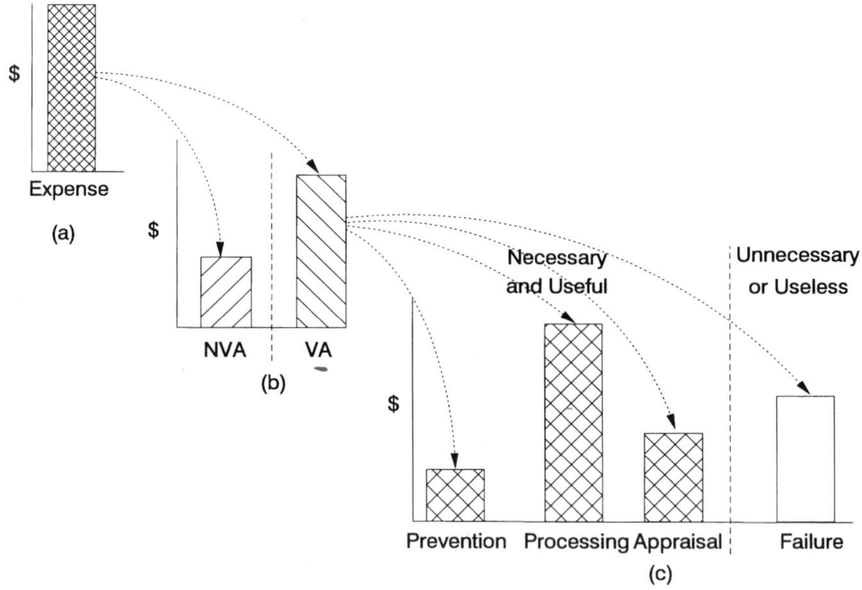

FIGURE 7.2 COQ Accounting Analysis of Salaries

it is based on assigning resources to activities assigned to cost objects. For example, rather than assume via a standard cost for direct nursing costs that all patients in the same unit use the same distribution of RNs, LPNs, and NAs, ABC tracks and assigns each type of nursing cost by patient. Value-added analysis does not assume that an equivalent amount of resource always provides the same value. Salaries can be separated into two bars (see Figure 7.2b): One, for salaries used for value-added activities, and the other for salaries used for non-value-added activities. The cost-of-quality analysis does not assume that each dollar spent on the same type of resource is used the same way. The value-added activities bar can then be separated into four categories (see Figure 7.2c), depending on whether the value-added salary was used for processing, appraisal, failure, or prevention. Failure to understand these differences creates obstacles to reducing operating costs by improving quality and delivery.

STATISTICAL SKILLS

In chapter 3, we learned that understanding processes was the key to continuous improvement. We have opportunities to improve because processes are repetitive. We can improve because processes vary, resulting in differences in quality, delivery, and cost (QDC). Variation causes nonconformance or defects. Statistics is a tool specifically designed for understanding variation and for correcting and preventing defects (see Figure 7.3). Two kinds of statistical analyses that are critical for continuous improvement are to estimate how much nonconformance exists (enumerative statistics) and to identify the sources or causes of the existing nonconformances (analytic statistics).[1] This should sound familiar as a different way posing Q1 and Q2. Each of these is discussed in the following sections.

---

1. Deming, W.E. "On the Distinction Between Enumerative and Analytical Surveys," *Journal of the American Statistical Association* 1953;48:244–55.

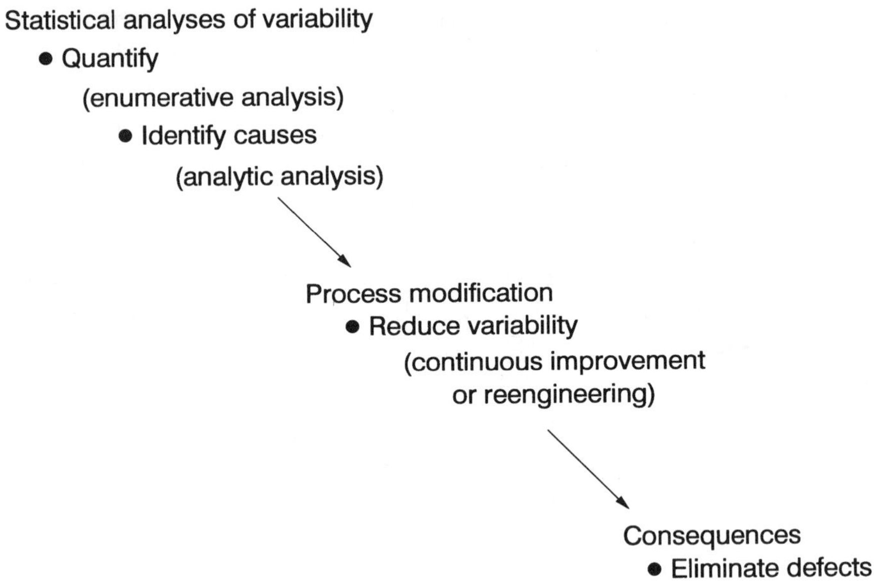

FIGURE 7.3 The Role of Statistics in Reducing Variability

Enumerative statistics

The word enumerative comes from the word enumerate, which means to count. Determining the quality, delivery, and cost levels for a particular process is a type of enumeration. You are counting the number of nonconformances, the days, hours, minutes, or seconds it takes to do an activity, or the dollars spent on using a resource. When counting you can use absolute numbers (e.g., patient days, number of mortalities, and dollars) or percentages (e.g., the percentage of total costs spent on failure costs or the percentage of patients who had extended lengths of stay for a particular DRG).

Enumerative statistics is used in appraisals and processing costs (e.g., by establishing baselines for QDC levels). These statistics are useful in identifying the different types of nonconformances and listing the reasons for undesirable outcomes. Enumerative statistics are connected to the appraisal and processing cost-of-quality categories. They also appear as part of problem solving in confirming that a solution works. The following are examples of enumerative statistics:

- Infant mortality rate in your community or at your organization.
- Number of caesarean sections.
- Number of outstanding receivables.
- Amount of payables overdue by 15 days.
- Laboratory supplies inventory.
- Number of beds per 1,000 in your community.
- Number of critical-care days per average length of stay.
- Which DRGs account for 80 percent of revenues.
- The types of claims being rejected.
- Length of time it takes registered patients to reach their hospital bed.
- Amount of hospital expenditures per capita.
- Which supplies take more than a week to be ordered.

Ideally, each output of a process would be analyzed to determine if it conforms to the customer's needs and requirements. Often, however, such analysis would be too costly. Testing may be destructive, there may be too many units to test, it would take too long to test, or the results would be unknown for some time. In such cases, taking a sample gives us an idea. But a sample cannot be too large because we would still have prohibitive costs, and it cannot be too small because then it would not be very informative.

Statistical process control (SPC) is a useful compromise between cost and information when compared with 100 percent inspection or to correcting defects discovered by the customer. With SPC, small samples are taken over a period of time. If the samples are similar with respect to conformance, they can be pooled together to get a more accurate estimate of the number of nonconformances. A statistical control chart can signal whether the samples are sufficiently similar enough to be pooled in this way. This larger, pooled sample yields more reliable estimates of the frequency of nonconformances.

When using SPC, however, do not forget that the initial purpose of doing an enumerative study is to determine the frequency of nonconformance. So, do not stop after determining that the samples are similar enough. From a process perspective, the samples are similar enough statistically if they behave in a stable manner, where stable is defined by statistical limits. Knowing a process is statistically stable, however, is well short of continuously improving. First, a statistically stable process may be consistently producing a 100 percent defective product or service! Second, a statistically stable process by itself does not provide any information of what the cause of the nonconformance is. Third, keeping a process statistically stable does not improve quality, delivery, or cost.

For example, Figure 7.4 shows a measure of nonconformance, the ratio of observed length of stay over expected length of stay, for several physicians. Notice first that physicians M.D.5 and M.D.16 are *statistically* different from the other physicians. There could be a variety of reasons for this variation (e.g., variations in practice patterns or setups). For our purposes, however, this process could be made stable in at least two ways: these two physicians could change their patterns so they are more like the others, or the others could change to be more like them. In both cases, the process could be stabilized statistically, but surely the latter solution is worse for the patient, employees, and the hospital. Also, 60 percent of the physicians have ratios exceeding 1.0. So, even those who are similar to the main group have ratios that exceed the standard.

Finally, if physician M.D.5 had one patient whose length of stay (LOS) exceeded the expected by a factor of 10, a con-

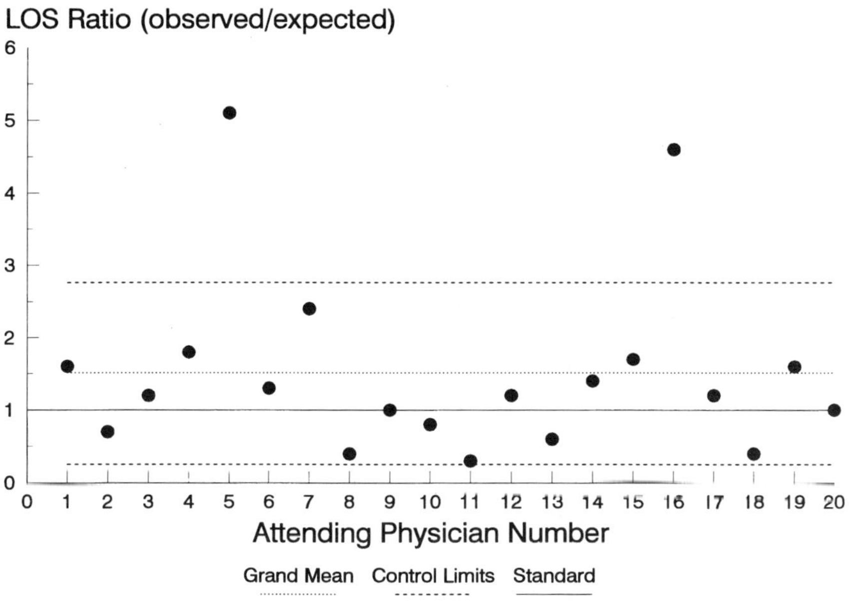

FIGURE 7.4 Measure of Nonconformance

trol chart is not necessary to know that understanding that patient's *causes* for the extended LOS could be worthwhile in reducing everyone's LOS ratio.

Analytic statistics

Analytic statistics is the kind of statistics used to determine what caused something or why something happened. The particular studies with which analytic statistics are useful are called designed experiments. Analytical statistics are useful for corrective and preventive actions. So, they typically occur with activities related to failure and prevention costs. The following are examples of analytic statistics:

- Why all children under two years old in your community are not immunized.
- How overdosing can be reduced.

- Why patients diagnosed under DRG 89 have extended lengths of stay.
- How surgical patients avoid delays.
- Why claims are being denied.
- Why some suppliers are easier to contact for preventive maintenance.
- Why patients take up to three hours from registration to reach their hospital bed.
- How patients can be admitted in half the time it now takes.
- Why a 3 p.m.-ordered blood test cannot be done until the following morning.
- How employee turnover can be reduced.

Analytic statistics are typically done by using experimental designs. Statisticians have developed designs for studies that reveal information readily because they are logically based. By understanding the logic behind the design, the user can interpret the data quickly. The interpretations are clues about which sources of variability have contributed to the nonconformance.

For example, to determine how many patients were diagnosed as DRG 107 for the first quarter of the year is an enumerative analysis. Data are collected from medical records to estimate the number. This number can also be expressed as a proportion or percent (e.g., as a percent of all patients). This is an enumerative statistical analysis. Studies of this type are often done by collecting a random sample and determining the count or proportion in the sample.

Analytic statistics help determine or confirm what factors caused a particular effect. For example, if you wanted to discover the factors that caused 17 percent of DRG 107 patients to exceed Medicare's allowable length of stay, you would perform an analytic study. This study could consist of controlling some factors and trying different combinations of others to see which contributed to the extended lengths of stay. The result of this analytic statistical analysis is a set of factors (e.g., delays in laboratory test results, lost orders, billing errors, comorbidities, and unsuccessful interventions), which could then be correlated with the extended length of stay. You would then see what changes you can make in the process to reduce the effect of these factors on extended lengths of stay. For example, you may need to find ways to reduce the number of lost orders or to reduce the laboratory turnaround time for lab results. Or, you could use a Pareto analysis to order these factors by degree of impact on patient outcome, satisfaction, and cost and attempt to eliminate the largest impacting factor.

LEARNING SKILLS

Without knowledge, improving continuously is impossible. Process knowledge comes from learning (e.g., that lost orders contributed to extended lengths of stay and why lost orders occur). The purpose of learning is to be able to predict outcomes of the process.[2] Being able to predict gives you the power to control the process. By controlling circumstances, you can control quality, delivery, and costs. For example, by reducing the number of lost orders because you change the probability of a lost order occurring, your predictions about extended length of stay improve.

One of the essential attributes of organizations that practice quality organizationwide is their ability to learn.[3] Learning organizations acquire two types of knowledge: factual and conceptual. They first learn *what* has occurred or is happening and then they learn *why* it occurred. These two types of learning are intimately connected to the two types of sta-

2. Deming, W.E. *The New Economics.* Cambridge: MIT Center for Advanced Engineering Technology, 1992, chapter 4.

3. Senge, P. *The Fifth Discipline.* New York: Doubleday, 1990.

tistical analyses. Enumerative analyses yield factual information by answering "What?" or "How much?" Analytic analyses yield conceptual information by answering "Why?" or "How?" Factual learning tells you to what degree you have control, while conceptual learning tells you how or what to control.

Learning by itself will not help reduce costs by improving quality and delivery. Factual and conceptual learning also goes through a use cycle. Factual learning helps in using standard procedures. Conceptual learning helps in creating new procedures. For example, all the people involved in the process for DRG 107 knew the facts about the procedures and applied those procedures. However, different circumstances occasionally arose for which the procedures were inadequate. Understanding the concepts behind the process is required to make changes in the procedure.

Just as there is cycle time efficiency for business-, employee-, and patient-focused processes, there is also cycle time efficiency for learning because learning is a process.[4] Organizations typically have extremely low efficiencies for learning cycle time. Learning requires going from awareness of a problem or opportunity, to learning something new about it, to using that knowledge to make a change that results in a verifiable improvement (see Figure 7.5). The time it takes to go from relative ignorance to knowledge is the learning cycle time, which includes the time to detect, correct, and verify.

For example, a patient complains about a long wait at admissions to an employee of the healthcare organization providing the services. The question for the organization is: How long does it take before the patient-focused process is changed? If the employee is not empowered to make an improvement, then in one sense the organization has not even advanced from ignorance to awareness. When the organiza-

4. Swartz, J. *Design of World-Class Operations.* Kokomo, IN: Competitive Actions, Inc., 1989.

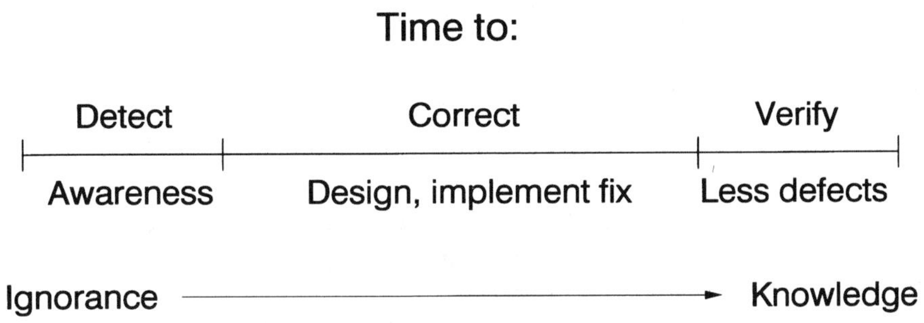

FIGURE 7.5 Learning Cycle Time

tion does become aware, how much time passes before it designs and implements a solution, and verifies the solution does work?

For many organizations, the total time is weeks, months, or years.

PROBLEM-SOLVING SKILLS

The five key elements of problem solving are:

1. Defining the problem (establishing a baseline).
2. Identifying the cause.
3. Developing a solution.
4. Confirming the solution.
5. Implementing the solution.

As shown in Table 7.1, these steps follow the Shewhart plan-do-check-act cycle.

Statistical and learning skills play vital roles in problem solving (see Figure 7.6). Enumerative statistics are used in defining the problem, confirming the solution, and implementing the solution because the data needed is collected by counting. For example, the percentage of medication errors before problem solving defines a problem, during problem

TABLE 7.1. Problem-Solving Procedure

STEP NUMBER	STEP	OBJECTIVE
1	Plan	To have a well-defined problem, objective, and valid measuring system for it.
2		To have a potential solution for a root cause (identified with data), a procedure for implementing it, and an idea of its cost and benefit.
3	Do	To have tried the well-defined, potential solution.
4	Check	To have data to verify the solution works or does not work.
5	Act	To have an improved process and ideas for the next improvement project.

Problem Solving	Statistics	Learning
Define problem	Enumerative	Factual
Identify cause	Analytic	Conceptual
Develop solution	Analytic	Conceptual
Confirm solution	Enumerative	Factual
Implement solution	Enumerative	Factual

FIGURE 7.6 Problem-Solving Skills

solving confirms whether a particular solution is effective, and after problem solving, such as in a control chart, helps implement the solution. Factual learning is required in these steps.

In identifying the root cause and in developing a solution, analytic statistics is required because the kind of knowledge needed is conceptual. For example, generating a list of potential causes of medication errors from which the root cause is determined requires a detailed understanding of the process. Similarly, once the root cause has been confirmed, developing an effective process change to eliminate or reduce the effect of the root cause requires a conceptual understanding of the process. Conceptual knowledge is knowledge about the causal relationships, which is required for elements two and three of problem solving.

Problem solving is useful for corrective and preventive actions. In corrective actions, the cost of problem solving is charged to failure costs because you are solving the immediate failure. In preventive actions, the cost of problem solving is charged to preventive costs because you will modify the process to avoid the failure in all future results. Corrective actions do not solve future problems, and preventive actions do not solve or correct the immediate (or past) failure.

The key to problem solving is in clearly stating the problem. Looking at problem solving as a double-funnel (see Figure 7.7) helps in progressing from a vague statement, to finding root causes, to maximizing the benefits of your solutions. Typically, you start problem solving by being aware of an undesirable symptom. This symptom is usually expressed in a vague and general way, for example, the vice-president of nursing's concern that "the nursing staff morale is low."

Defining key words of this vague statement helps focus on the specific problem. Key words are the nouns and verbs of the general statement describing the symptom. The vice-president of nursing determined that the key words were *nursing staff* and *morale*. By talking with her staff, she defined the nursing staff as the RNs with more than two years of ex-

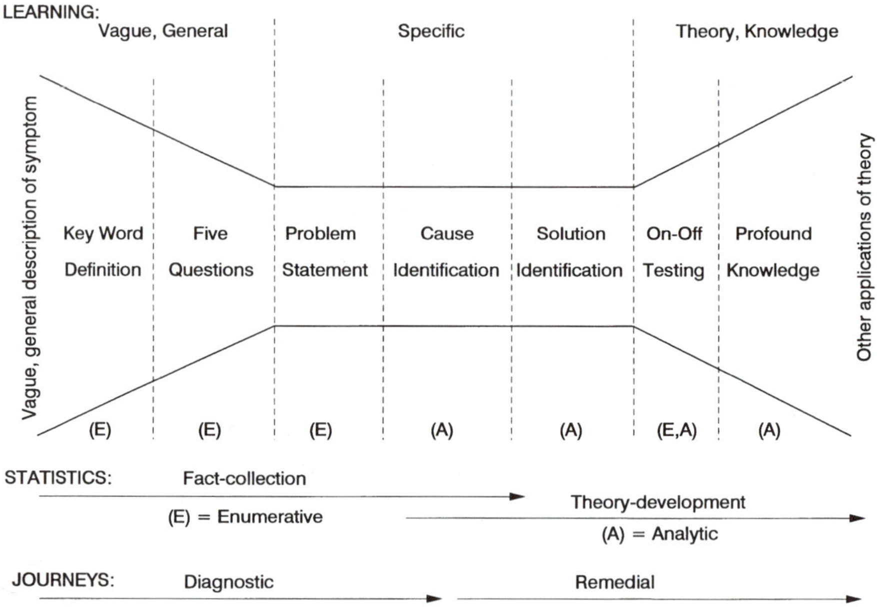

FIGURE 7.7 Double-Funnel Approach to Problem Solving

perience at the hospital. These nurses were complaining specifically about having to do tasks that they felt were not professional tasks, requiring the skills of a registered nurse. This information contributed to a significant focusing of the problem statement.

There are five questions that also help in fine-tuning the problem statement: Who?, What?, Where?, When?, and How much? By adding data to support the statement, the vague and general awareness of a symptom becomes a specific and data-supported statement of a problem and establishes a baseline for comparison. The vice-president of nursing assigned one of her administrative staff to initiate a data-collection procedure. She wanted to know what specific tasks the RNs thought did not require their professional skills, when and where were they doing these tasks, and how much time these tasks took during their 12-hour shifts. This became one operational definition of "nursing morale staff is low:" over a

TABLE 7.2. Patient-Focused Problem Statement

QUESTION	ANSWER
WHO?	Patients.
WHAT?	Being discomforted and inconvenienced and experiencing lost-work time and lost family-time because of delays.
WHERE?	At admissions.
WHEN?	After registering.
HOW MUCH?	An average of 41 minutes.

three-month period, the RNs did any several of 15 specific tasks at any time during their shift that occupied an average of 2.75 hours per 12-hour shift.

The key to using problem solving with cost of quality and value-added analysis, is in defining problems or opportunities for improvement (failures) from the patient's perspective (for PVA processes). A patient-focused problem statement already has the first question answered generically: the patient is who (see Table 7.2). Analogous problem statements are developed for solving BVA and EVA process problems.

Recall from chapter 2 that none of the organizations involved in the National Demonstration Project tackled patient care directly. Another survey from Coopers & Lybrand also reported that while the hospitals reporting in the survey on the average decreased costs by 23 percent, laboratory test turnaround time by 50 percent, and patient registration time by 80 percent, there is no clear evidence that these improvements resulted in improved patient care.[5]

5. "Quality Watch," *Hospitals* December 20, 1991.

Now the vice-president of nursing wanted their problem statement restated in terms of the impact it had on patients. She and the RN unit managers identified several undesirable consequences: patients complained of not having enough personal attention from the nurses, the instructions provided from the nurses seemed hurried at times, making the patients less likely to listen and understand, and patients were more likely to wait for certain nursing care. Initially, the vice-president of nursing thought they had regressed rather than made progress, having returned to vague and general statements. However, by designing a data-collection procedure, they could identify and quantify the frequency and duration of these consequences.

Finding the root cause ends what Juran calls the diagnostic journey in problem solving.[6] The remedial journey then begins. A solution is a way of eliminating the root cause or the root cause's effect. This is confirmed by on-off testing: you must be able to reproduce the effect (on) and its elimination (off). By understanding the relationship between the root cause and the solution in a theoretical way, you are then able to generalize the solution and apply it in other similar situations.

Enumerative statistics and factual learning are required in defining the problem (see Table 7.3). Because continuous improvement is based on data, you need to know the degree of poor quality, delivery and costs. That degree can be expressed as the number, proportion, or percentage of times quality is poor, delivery is late, or costs are too high. It can also be expressed in other units (e.g., morbidity or mortality rates, hours, or dollars). By collecting data and analyzing them appropriately, you learn what your current or new quality, delivery, and costs are. Enumerative analyses also play a role in the fourth element: confirming the solution's effectiveness. This means estimating the new quality, delivery, and cost levels and comparing them with the old levels.

Analytic studies are useful for identifying the cause (as shown in Table 7.3). The cause is a factor or factors that contribute to the poor results in quality, delivery, or cost. This is

6. Juran, J.M. *Juran on Planning for Quality.* New York: The Free Press, 1988.

TABLE 7.3. Integration of Statistics, Learning, Problem-Solving, and Cost Management

DISCIPLINE	APPLICATION: What? How much?	APPLICATION: Why? How?
Statistics	Enumerative: estimation of probabilities	Analytic: identification of causes
Learning	Factual	Conceptual
Problem solving	No	Yes
Cost of quality Categories	• Processing • Appraisal	• Failure • Prevention

the type of answer needed to the question *How* can the quality, delivery, and cost levels be improved? By collecting data and analyzing it appropriately, you learn which factors are the cause. In developing a solution, analytic studies increase your knowledge about the causal relationship between the identified factor and the improved performance.

The role of statistics in problem solving is illustrated in Figure 7.8. Starting with enumerative statistics from an enumerative study, the types (d_1 through d_k) and frequencies (amounts) of defects or nonconformances are enumerated for each cycle of the process (units of repetition). By using a Pareto chart (following the first arrow clockwise) and ranking the types from most frequent to least, the opportunity for the greatest improvement is identified as the one with the largest bar. A cause-and-effect diagram (next arrow) is then used to identify the potential causes of this type of defect. A hypothesis is developed that explains why one or more of the potential causes is the actual root cause. This is tested using an experiment in which certain factors are controlled, which is an analytic study. The analysis of the data to identify the root causes is an analytic analysis.

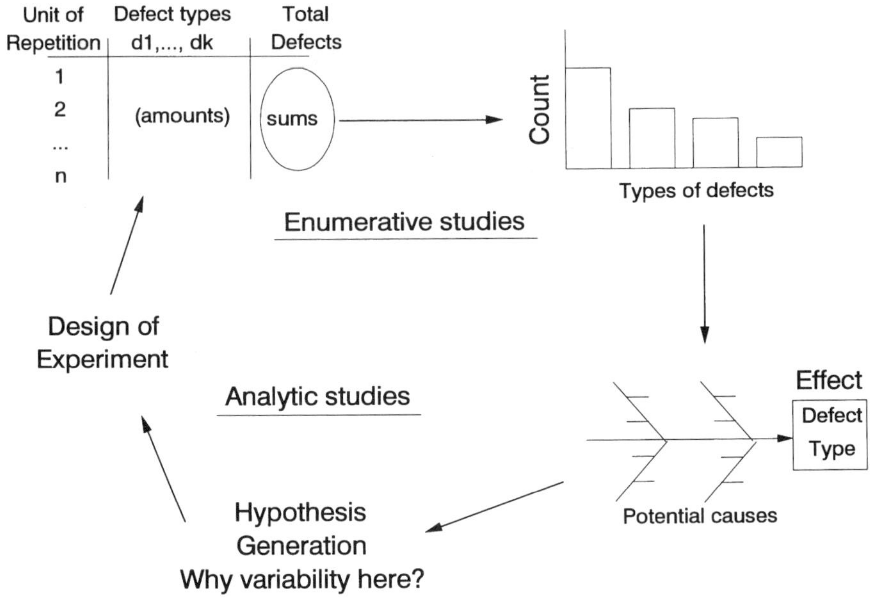

FIGURE 7.8 The Role of Statistics in Problem Solving

The first enumerative study as depicted by the defect table in Figure 7.8 answers the question:What are the current quality, delivery, and cost levels? The Pareto chart organizes the answer so that makes it clear where the greatest opportunity is for improvement. Starting with the cause-and-effect diagram through the designed experiment, these analyses lay the foundation to answer the question: *How* can these levels be improved?

PVA EXAMPLE: PATIENTS COMPLAIN OF LONG WAITS BEFORE SERVICE

Old situation

Figure 7.9 describes the circumstances when there is no information and no learning by an organization. This culture fosters a negative attitude in patients and employees. People infer attitudes from behaviors. For example, when patients

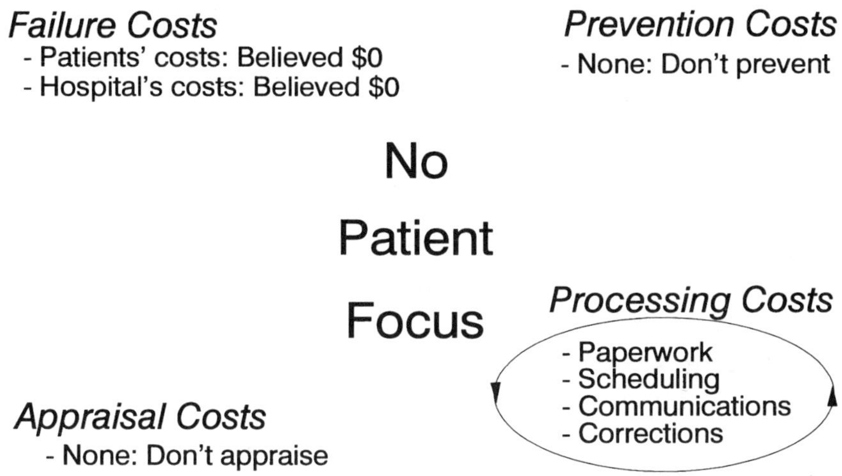

FIGURE 7.9 No Information, No Learning

complain at admissions of long delays, and the hospital does not appear responsive, patients infer that the hospital does not care. In particular, they judge the hospital as not being patient focused. The question What is the current quality level of admissions?, is not asked, so there is no answer. The patients have one opinion; the hospital another. Within the hospital, administration has one opinion and the admission's clerk has another.

What is the cost of appraisal? $0. Not one penny is spent in determining the current quality level. Are there data? There are data on times of arrival and times of attendance by a hospital employee (clerk, nurse, and physician). But there is no learning from these data because the question about current quality level is not asked.

Are there failure costs? From the hospital's behavior—not asking if patients are satisfied with the waits, much less improving the situation—the community can and does infer that the hospital believes the cost to them is $0. Asking this question places the hospital in a difficult situation. If the cost is $0, the community may infer that because it does not cost the hospital anything, it is not interested in improving community relations through reduced waiting times. Or, if the hospital does know what its cost is, it raises the question of why it doesn't do something about it rather than wasting money.

Because the hospital never asks about current levels, it never gets to ask how to improve those levels. There are no prevention costs, but there are costs for all the activities associated with this process. However, these costs are unknown. It is possible to estimate them, but no one has. Fig. 7.9 describes the situation without continuous improvement, without learning, without facts, without knowledge.

This system failed at all five objectives of an appraisal process (see chapter 4):

1. There were no estimates of quality and costs.
2. It did not assess patient satisfaction.
3. There were no data recorded.
4. It did not lead to corrective or preventive action.
5. It was a long time before an improvement was made.

New situation

The hospital implements a quality management philosophy and assigns a quality improvement team to improve community relations, starting with the hospital-patient relations at admissions (see Figure 7.10). The hospital asks, What is the current quality level at admissions with respect to patient satisfaction? The team collects data over a three-month period. Among the data collected are:

- Patients waited from 17 minutes to 129 minutes with an average of 44 minutes.
- The admitting clerk and patient must handle seven forms.
- Patients rate the wait an average of 1.9 on a scale of 5 = completely satisfied to 1 = completely dissatisfied.

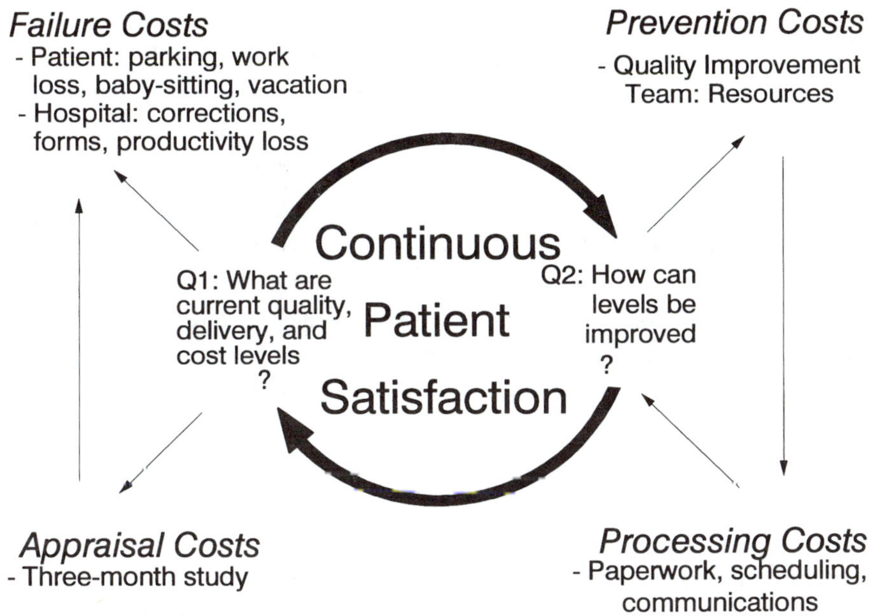

FIGURE 7.10 Hospital-Patient Relations

The answer Q1 is enumerative in either minutes, dollars, forms, number of patient concerns, or dissatisfaction level. The cost of this study is charged to appraisal costs.

The team still cannot estimate the cost of failure. The team believes with the information they have, that it may be some amount, but they are unable to quantify it because they do not know what to measure. However, the three-month study did reveal to them that there was a failure cost that they did not incur but their patients did. Patients reported that the delays made them incur additional costs (e.g., parking fees, baby-sitting fees, loss of vacation time, loss of productivity). The team was not aware that some patients were forced to take vacation time and that a half-hour delay could mean an extra half-day of vacation used. The team decided that there was an unknown amount greater than $0 of failure cost incurred by their patients along with their dissatisfaction level.

The team answered question Q2: how to improve these levels through problem solving. The problem statement was developed by defining key words and answering five questions: Who? What? When? Where? and How much? The key to recognizing that a patient problem existed was in stating the impact of delays on the patient. The team had facts to make a statement from the patient's perspective (see Table 7.2).

By using various problem-solving tools, the team was able to generate a solution with two key features: they replaced the seven forms with one that was simpler to read, understand, and fill out; they arranged to preadmit patients. The cost of developing, designing, and implementing the solution is charged to prevention costs.

There are new activities associated with the process and the cost of the new process can be compared with the old process cost. A review showed savings in the tens of thousands of dollars due to improved cash flow, reduced number of errors at admissions, and fewer forms. There were, after all, failure costs incurred by the hospital that the hospital did not know about. Ignorance did not make these costs vanish—learning did.

There was factual learning. The team learned through enumerative statistical analyses the amount of delays, the types of costs patients incurred because of the delays, the level of dissatisfaction, and that there were failure costs that the hospital incurred (e.g., paperwork, materials, correction of errors, poor scheduling, and productivity loss). The team also acquired conceptual learning. They learned that there were two key root causes of the delays: the number of forms and the verification of insurance. Initially, it was believed there were no failure costs. This belief was not based on data. Data revealed that it is ignorance that incurs costs.

They leveraged this solution by realizing five consequences:

1. Collecting data is essential to improvement.
2. Data-collection without learning and action is a wasted cost.

3. There are two types of knowledge with different purposes.
4. Learning what the levels of quality and costs are is different from knowing how to improve them.
5. Improving patient satisfaction can lead to improved organizational efficiency, effectiveness, and adaptability.

8 Cycle Time Management: Reducing Quality and Delivery Costs

Value-based cost management integrates activity-based costing, value-added analysis, and cost of quality with the continuous improvement cycle. The senior executive of chapter 1 can use this integration to answer the question: How can everyone reduce costs by improving quality and delivery?

Using the Continuous Improvement Cycle System (CICS) as shown in Figure 7.1 to reduce costs by improving quality and delivery is simple:

- Just select a process you want to improve.
- Then apply the CICS by:
  —answering Q1: What are the current quality, delivery, and cost levels? to establish a baseline, and
  —answering Q2: How can these levels be improved? to improve.

Of course, answering each question requires much work and learning and extensive use of your CICS skills. In addition, selecting a process requires some thought and planning to make the selections worthwhile. Cycle time management is the key to organizing the integration of activity-based costing (ABC), value-added analysis (VAA), and cost of quality (COQ) for more effective and efficient use of the CICS. It provides a logical approach to reducing costs by improving quality and delivery.

CYCLE TIME MANAGEMENT

Time, quality, and cost are critical factors for all businesses. Managing them has traditionally been difficult because they are viewed as opposing forces. Trade-offs must be made: faster means risking quality; higher quality means higher costs. As with most problems, solutions can be found in specific definitions—in this case, of time and quality.

Recall that processes are the key to continuous improvement because they offer an opportunity to improve through their repetitiveness. This is the clue to how cycle time management can actually provide better quality. Reducing cycle time increases the number of opportunities to improve over a given period because the time it takes to complete a process is shortened. With more opportunities, more improvement is possible. For example, increasing the number of times in a given period you cycle through the CICS automatically results in improved quality. In healthcare, cycle time reduction also reduces labor costs, which is critical since nearly two-thirds of the typical hospital's expenses are labor.

Cycle time reduction reduces the time to deliver a service. This in turn increases the potential for higher productivity. Since many costs are influenced by volume, increasing productivity reduces the cost per unit of service. Overhead costs are then spread across more service units, reducing their percentage of the total cost of that service unit.

In addition, reduction of cycle time creates opportunities for other process activities to be improved by helping point out their weaknesses. Processes typically become bureaucratic because of delays. Additional steps are added to compensate for the delays in in-between or intermediate services. By having to respond more quickly, the inherent flaws in the process are revealed.

Using Juran's sense of quality, freedom from deficiencies means that improving quality reduces costs through less rework. Cycle time management eliminates the need for trade-offs to manage time, quality, and costs by paving the way for improving quality through continuous improvement and reducing costs through reduction in deficiencies and labor costs per process cycle. The ability to manage cycle time requires an awareness of time and an ability to focus on the factors that increase cycle time. In chapter 5 we saw that these factors consist of transportation, queuing, delays, storage, waits, and so on. These need to be eliminated through problem-solving skills.

Cycle time management is applicable to all processes and systems. For example, from a business value-added perspective rejection of reimbursement submission increases the cash flow cycle time that reduces the value-added to the business. Delays in solving employee issues reduce the value added through employee value-added processes. For example, annual employee evaluations severely limit the value of the feedback.

SELECT A PROCESS TO IMPROVE

There are three types of processes that can be selected: patient-focused, employee-focused, or business-focused. From total quality management's two basic principles, businesses must profit from satisfying customers and people are an organization's greatest asset, it follows that three types of value are added according to Figure 8.1. The organization must first add value to employees because they add value to patients and other stakeholders, who consequently add value to the business.

Another cycle appears, to which cycle time management is applicable. The sooner the organization can increase employee value, the sooner employees can increase patient value, who will in turn increase business value that much sooner.

Processes can also be selected by their scope. Management should focus on systems (senior management) and processes (middle management) that add value to employees. Quality improvement teams should focus on patient value-added processes. Individuals should focus on their

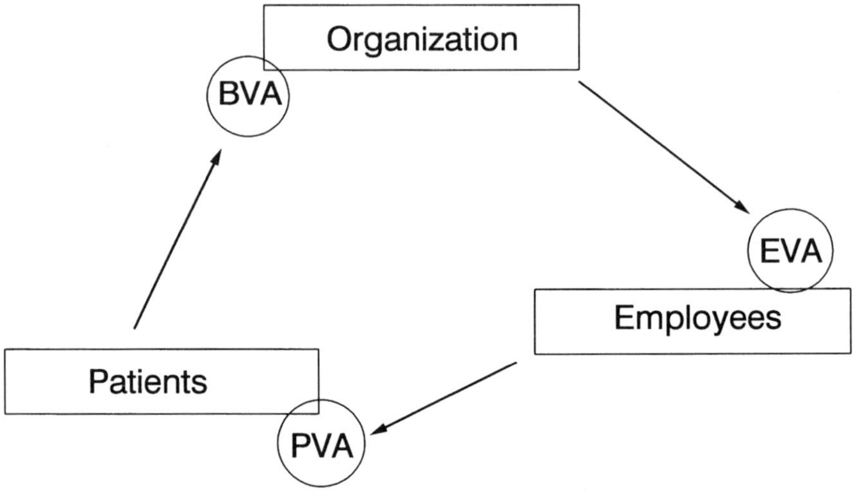

FIGURE 8.1 Three Types of Value and Their Interdependencies

own processes in a way that supports the management's system selection by having specific missions and goals defined with their management. Everyone uses the same skills as defined by the CICS.

For example, a patient-focused quality-improvement team consisting of representatives from nursing, pharmacy, dietetics, and the clinical laboratory may decide to look at malnutrition because of the JCAHO change in standards requiring such a focus. Everyone on the team has had training on the CICS skills. Together, they realized that the double-funnel requires them to first narrowly focus on a specific problem and then use their knowledge gained from solving that problem to generalize to similar problems. They identify potential candidates as hospitalized patients whose primary diagnosis will require them to forego food for more than four to five days because of the diagnostic or therapeutic procedure. At their hospital, this meant looking at patients diagnosed for:

- Intestinal/abdominal surgery.
- Carcinomas/lymphomas.

- Peripheral vascular disease.
- Pneumonia or respiratory infection.
- Orthopedic surgery.

They decided to look more closely at patients undergoing elective GI surgery. What they learn from these processes they intend to apply first to other types of surgery (e.g., colorectal resections) and then to the other types of processes listed (e.g., for carcinomas and inflammatory disease).

APPLYING THE CICS

To apply the CICS, you will need to determine measures for quality, delivery, and costs of the process you selected. This may seem a daunting task because in the previous chapters several different kinds of measures were identified: measures on outcomes associated with value; measures on processes associated with performance and improvement; and measures on cost associated with quality.

You can organize these measures in two ways. One way is to organize them from a process-outcome perspective. The three process measures effectiveness, efficiency, and adaptability are process or P-criteria.[1] The six measures of value listed in Table 5.1 are results (outcome) or R-criteria. Figure 8.2 shows the relationships among the patient (cost object), process performance (P-criteria), and outcomes (R-criteria).

By recognizing different types of patients, you expect to design, manage, and control the P-criteria to effect particular R-criteria values: patient satisfaction and clinical outcome (PVA processes), work environment and employee satisfaction (EVA processes), financial and operational performance (BVA processes). Unfortunately, P-criteria do not directly cause R-criteria values. You can establish only a correlation

1. Imai, Masaaki. *Kaizen: The Key to Japan's Competitive Success.* Milwaukee, WI: Quality Bookshelf Press, 1986.

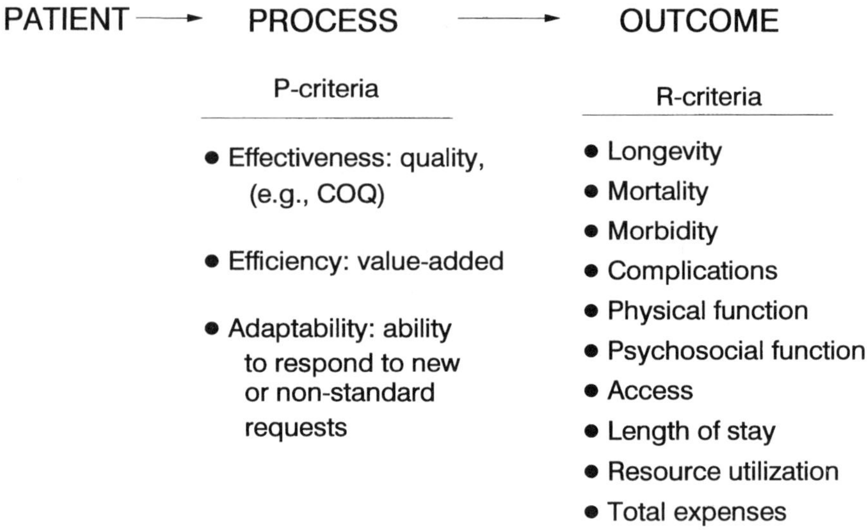

FIGURE 8.2 Relationships Among the Patient, Process, and Outcome

between P-criteria and R-criteria or between process measures and results.

The second way to organize the measures is by using the principle of cycle time management: time measures first, then quality measures, and finally costs. Of the three process measures (processes come before outcomes), efficiency and adaptability are time-related. Process quality is measured by effectiveness. Process effectiveness is incorporated into the four cost-of-quality categories. The COQ categories are also cost measures. In addition, failure costs consist of failing to meet the process measure expectations and failing to meet the outcome expectations.

In Table 8.1, this ordering of the measures is illustrated for the process selected by the malnutrition team. They began with the process measures efficiency and adaptability because they include time.

They then listed the cost-of-quality categories as quality or effectiveness process measures. This list required two columns: one for the baseline (which answers question about the current process levels of) and another for the new process

TABLE 8.1. Process and Outcome Measures for Protein-Calorie Malnutrition Study

TIME: EFFICIENCY AND ADAPTABILITY		
• Percentage of patients with PCM identified before surgery • Percentage of patients with ELOS due to PCM • Percentage of patients with inadequate feeding days		
COST OF QUALITY		
CATEGORY	**BASELINE**	**MODIFIED**
Prevention	Not applicable	Cost of start-up: • Creation of nutrition committee • Design and development of nutritional plan, pre-albumin testing, procedures, and audits • Training and education of admissions personnel
Processing	• Surgery	• Surgery • Pre-albumin test at admissions: reagents, quality control, instrument maintenance, labor, reportable result • Interdepartmental communications
Appraisal	• Status check after surgery • Initial review and analysis of surgery patients	• Status check after surgery • Periodic audits of nutritional program • Status check before surgery

TABLE 8.1. (*continued*)

COST OF QUALITY		
CATEGORY	**BASELINE**	**MODIFIED**
Failure (P-criteria)	Additional care due to PCM: • Postop inadequate feeding period • Weight/fat reserve loss • Infection at operative site • Postoperative wound dehiscence • Concentration of visceral proteins • Impaired immunological reserves	Additional care due to PCM: • Same as baseline plus • Testing process failure
VALUE ADDED: FROM PROCESS IMPROVEMENT		
• High risk patients identified at admissions • Decreased mortality/morbidity from PCM		• Decreased additional care due to PCM • ELOS reduced
CLINICAL OUTCOME MEASURES (R-CRITERIA)		
• Reoperation • Mortality	• Pneumonia • Physical and psychosocial functional status	• Septicemia

(the result of answering how to improve those levels is a modified process). There are no prevention costs assigned to the baseline because it is the unmodified process. The prevention costs for the modified process are those costs incurred to design, develop, and deliver the new process.

The processing costs are those costs incurred for using both current and modified processes.

The appraisal costs for the baseline process are those costs associated with determining what its impact was on poor quality. In the modified process, routine assessment costs to assess the effectiveness of the new process would be incurred and categorized as appraisal costs.

Failure costs are those costs associated with the process not meeting its objective. This requires two types of measures to support the relationship between processes and outcomes. Under failure costs in the COQ section of Table 8.1, only measures of process effectiveness (quality measures) are listed as efficiency; adaptability (time measures) were listed earlier under the time section.

The R-criteria were listed separately under clinical outcome measures. These are outcome measures for this patient value-added process. For example, quality control measures are P-criteria, while poor wound healing would be an R-criterion.

To understand what cost information they needed, the malnutrition team started with an overview flowchart of elective GI surgery, one of their candidate processes. They first drew a flowchart of the ideal process (see Figure 8.3): they denoted the flow by arrows, input and output by circles,

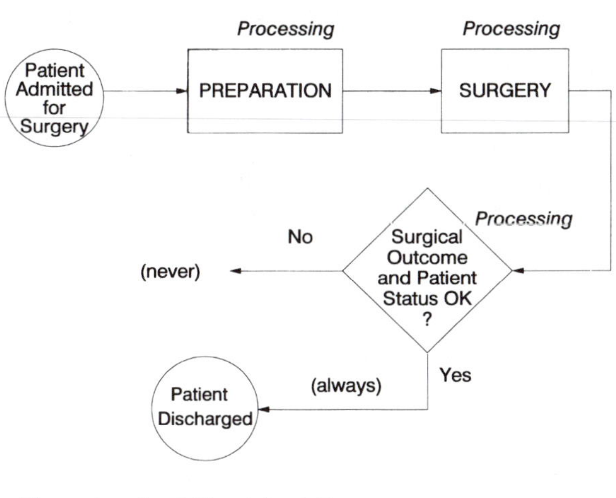

FIGURE 8.3 Flowchart of the Ideal Process

transformations by rectangles, and quality decisions to determine if the needs are met by diamonds.

The team then drew another flowchart to represent what actually occurred because they knew that "no" answers did occur at the diamond and there were delays, which they denoted by an ovule. They labeled the symbols with the COQ categories (see Figure 8.4). In comparing the two charts, they saw that finance viewed all expenses as processing expenses, while in reality some processing expenses were appraisal and failure expenses and some were non-value-added expenses.

Answering Q1: Establishing a baseline on quality, delivery, and cost levels

Recall that the message the senior executive of chapter 1 got from the different cases was that without measurement, you cannot be aware. Measurement also allows you to confirm that your changes were successful by comparing the results from the modified process to the baseline established before the process was modified.

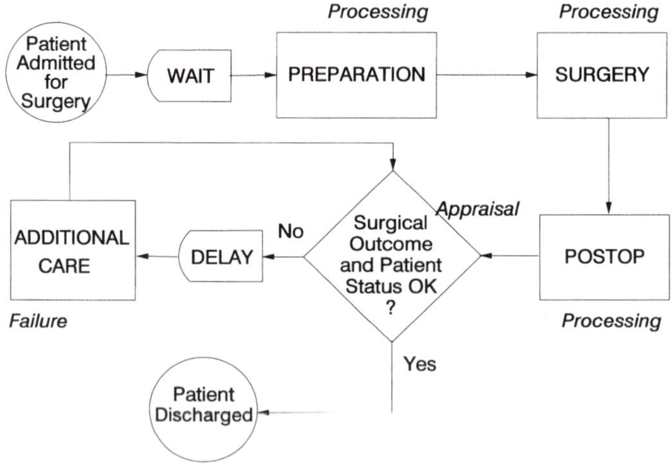

FIGURE 8.4 Flowchart of the Actual Process

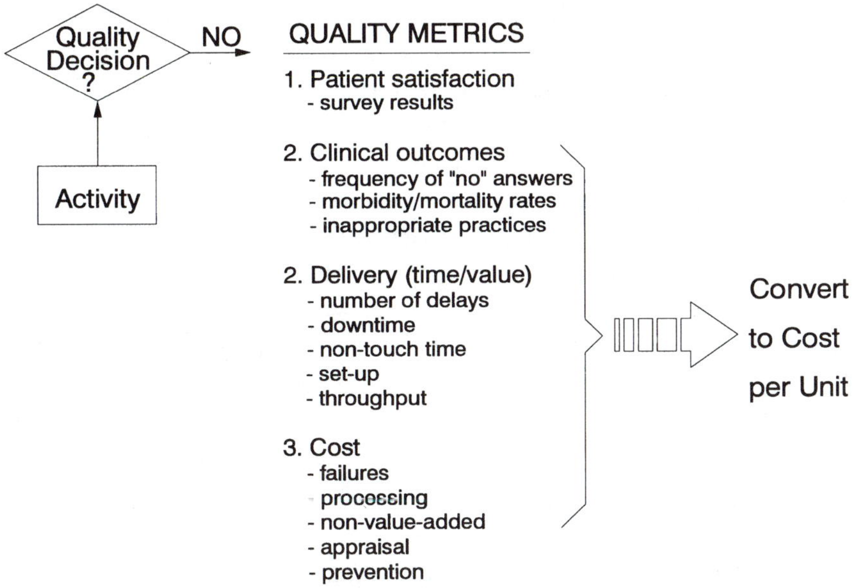

FIGURE 8.5 Flowchart of Quality Decision Points

Measuring quality can start at the quality decision points (appraisals) in your flowchart (see Figure 8.5). To paraphrase an old saying: diamonds are a customer's best friends because information on quality is collected here. Without quality decisions, you cannot collect data and therefore, you will be unable to answer Q1. The frequency of "no" answers and the types of nonconformances are enumerative statistics that are readily displayed in a Pareto chart.

The second flowchart indicated to the team that unintended outcomes occurred in the additional care activity box. From experience they knew that some patients had reoperations, came down with pneumonia and septicemia, were unable to function normally, and had increased morbidity due to poor quality of intervention. These activities created a demand for the additional care, which meant additional resources.

Identifying to which cost-of-quality category each activity belongs is critical to accurate cost estimation. Information on costs can be found by estimating the cost of the resources used at each rectangle (processing costs) in the flowchart of the process. In addition, you can estimate the cost of the resources at diamonds (appraisals) and corrective actions (typically rectangles following diamonds along the "no" path). Typically, these cost estimates will based on standard costs. Here is an opportunity to apply ABC to determine whether the traditional cost estimates will be accurate enough.

Delivery levels or times are determined from time estimates. Data on times are cycle times and processing times. Cycle time is the easiest to collect. Start the clock at the start circle (input) in the flowchart and stop the clock when you reach the end circle (output) in the chart. For example, length of stay is a measure of clinical process cycle time. The subprocesses (e.g., time to be admitted, time to be diagnosed, time to intervention, and time to receive payment) should also be tracked. Process time is the time spent on the processing activities (rectangles). The next step is to identify VA activities and NVA activities.

Decide how you will estimate costs, quality, and delivery for this process by developing an action plan that includes determining:

1. What measures you will use.
2. Who will make the measurements.
3. How the data will be collected and stored.
4. What analyses are needed.

For example, the malnutrition team generated several measurements of quality, cost, and delivery. Of 83 elective GI surgery patients they could get information on, they found that three (3.6 percent) underwent reoperation, potentially because of malnutrition causing wound dehiscence. They also found that another 17 patients (20.5 percent) had extended lengths of stay—ostensibly due to malnutrition. From finance, they found that the standard cost was $7,560 per patient, or for these 83 patients, $627,480. The actual expenses were $727,039, 16 percent higher. This indicated that perhaps as much as 16 percent of expenses were attributable to failure costs.

The medical technologist on the team extracted information from 74 of these patients on efficiency of the laboratory in producing lab results. She also drew a flowchart illustrating an overview of the laboratory process (see Figure 8.6) and labeled the activities using the COQ categories. She decided that order entry, quality control, run tests, and issue report were essential parts of the laboratory process. She estimated the time these activities took and compared it to the total time from receipt of specimen to the time the result was available for the physician. The laboratory's efficiency was 17.3 percent on average for these 74 patients.

Finance was unable to analyze further the standard cost to help the team estimate the costs for each cost-of-quality category. So, the team also collected data for the overall elective GI surgery process and developed a table to present this information. They highlighted the worst-case scenario by creating a table with its COQ estimates (see Figure 6.12). They re-

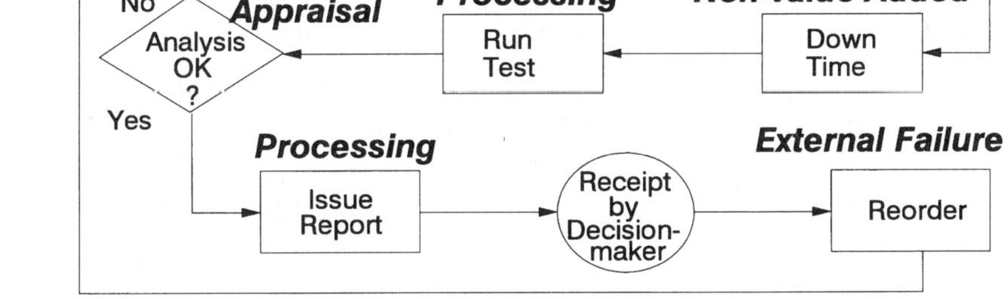

FIGURE 8.6 Flowchart of the Laboratory Process

alized that in this case, failure costs doubled the total expenses associated with treating the patient. Unfortunately, they also confirmed with finance that not all of those expenses were reimbursable, so there could easily be a net loss for the hospital with these patients.

Answering Q2: Reducing quality and delivery costs

Reducing costs begins with identifying opportunities. The size of the cost estimates is one way to identify opportunities. Actual expenses clearly showed an opportunity for the team to start reducing costs by improving quality and delivery.

Another way is to analyze the quality decision points or diamonds in process flowcharts. Every "no, this does not conform," is an opportunity to improve. You can construct several charts to show the results at the diamonds. A bar chart of the distribution of total process costs across the four cost-of-quality categories is one way to show the baseline you have established. Place the bars in the following order: prevention, processing, appraisal, and failure. For example, the team constructed a bar chart of their COQ estimates for the overall process (see Figure 8.7).

You can also construct two Pareto charts showing the different types of failures or nonconformances versus frequency for one chart and cost for the other. The team constructed a bar chart comparing the different reasons extended LOS occurred for the 83 patients (see Figure 8.8). Another possibility is to construct a Pareto chart of process activity versus time (amount of time per activity), and another versus cost. This information comes directly from the appraisal information. Each chart identifies an opportunity because they suggest that the category with the highest bar (first one in a Pareto chart) is one place to start reducing costs by improving quality and delivery.

For the malnutrition team, there was clearly an opportunity to improve the delivery and quality of patient care that

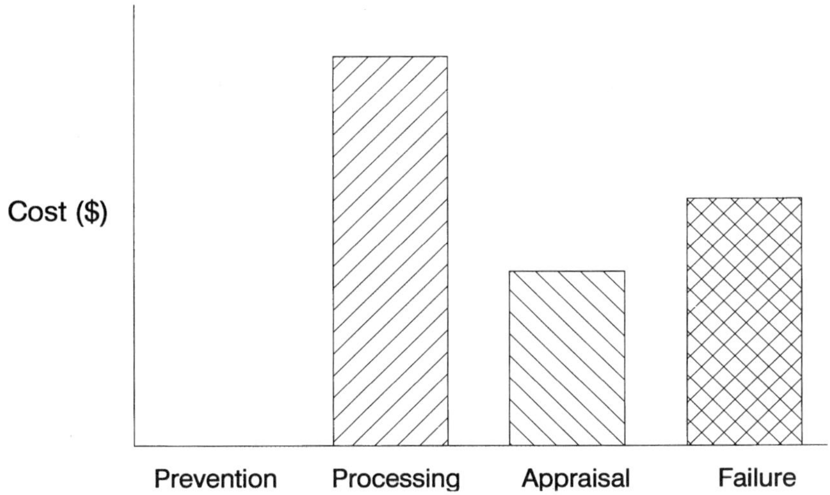

FIGURE 8.7 Bar Chart of COQ Estimates for the Overall Process

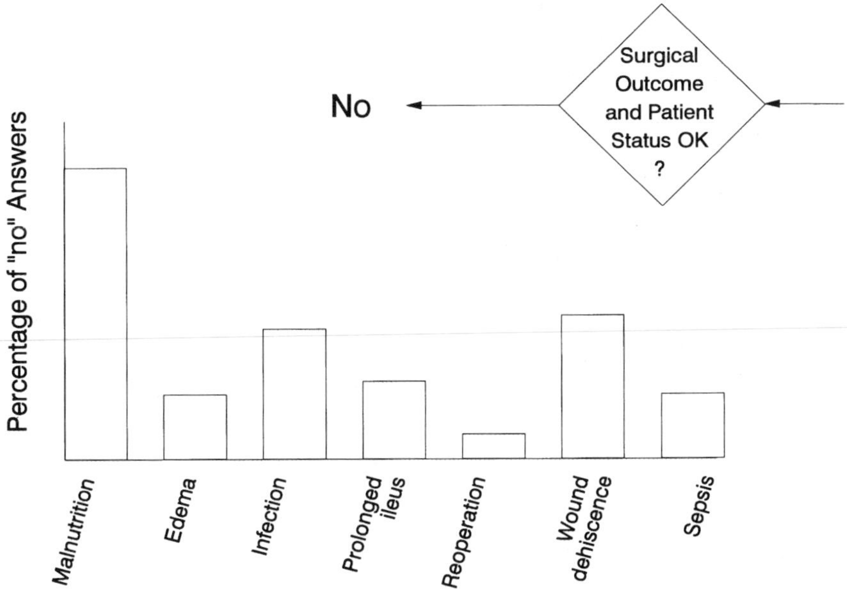

FIGURE 8.8 Reasons for Extended LOS

would result in reduced expenses for the hospital by identifying patients at risk for protein-calorie malnutrition (PCM) when their primary diagnosis was something else. Their cycle time management information in Table 8.1 confirmed what they already suspected: reducing the time it takes to identify at-risk patients was the key. Their measures of efficiency would confirm this with facts.

They developed a two-stage approach to process modification:

1. Identify at-risk patients for PCM with the facilitation of the laboratory.
2. Develop a multitiered nutritional intervention based on the risk level.

Each stage would involve a subcommittee of the team to develop and ensure that cross-functional issues would be resolved to the benefit of the patient. The goal was to optimize the total process, even if it meant suboptimization of one area.

The laboratory's approach included four roles:

1. Evaluation at admission.
2. Assessment of metabolic needs.
3. Response assessment.
4. Micronutrients assessment.

Each component would have a set of criteria used for classification and evaluation. Sampling of records for manual data analysis or summary statistics from an information system file would be used to assess the effectiveness of the program.

The department of clinical dietetics stratified patients according to their nutritional status:

- Level 1—adequate oral food intake.
- Level 2—need oral supplements and are at risk for nutritional status decline.

- Level 3—severely stressed and require specialized nutritional support.

Level-1 patients would be evaluated weekly, while level-2 and -3 patients more often. Level-3 patients would require enteral or parenteral feeding. They are malnourished either before hospitalization or because of their primary diagnosis or therapeutic procedure are unable to take oral food once hospitalized. The subcommittee consisted of the representatives from nursing, dietetics, and pharmacy to design, develop, and deliver the nutritional support program to address these patients.

The laboratory would establish a method for assessing the effectiveness of the program. They decided that they would address several areas in the assessment:

- Assessment and nutrition plan in 72 hours.
- Initiation of nutrition support.
- Monitors for support.
- Measure anabolic status.
- Transitional feeding.
- Discontinuation of support.
- Ineffective nutrition support.

To justify the cost of these efforts, the team also developed a table of COQ accounts (see Table 8.2). The cost of all their work to-date is assigned to prevention costs.

The team drew the overview flowchart for the modified process (see Figure 8.9). The new process has two more appraisals or quality decision points: an assessment at admissions to identify at-risk patients and an assessment during preop to determine the effectiveness of their preventive feeding program and averting PCM and its consequences for both the patient and the organization.

TABLE 8.2. Cost-of-Quality Accounting

ACCOUNT / TITLE	ACTIVITY	COST
100 **APPRAISAL**		
110 Outcome Audits:		
a. Manual chart review	a. Patients who underwent colorectal, gastric/esophageal, or intestinal resections for carcinoma and inflammatory diseases.	
b. Daily running total	b. Department of clinical dietetics audit for stratifying patients to three levels of malnourishment risk.	
200 **FAILURES**		
210 Quality or Delivery of Healthcare Results		
211 Clinical Outcomes	Additional care for: pneumonia, septicemia, fat reserve loss, muscle wasting, impaired immunological reserves, weight loss, low concentrations of visceral proteins, postoperative wound dehiscence, infections at operative site, postoperative period of inadequate feeding.	
220 Support Services		

TABLE 8.2. (*continued*)

ACCOUNT / TITLE	ACTIVITY	COST
221 Delayed Intervention or Institution of Oral Feeding	Resulting in: ELOS and increase of facility utilization and costs.	
300 **PREVENTION**		
310 Leadership		
311 Senior Executive Involvement	Creation and involvement of nutrition committee: review protocols and standards.	
320 Information and Analysis		
321 Information and Data Management	Development of indicators of at-risk patients, audits for evaluating program effectiveness.	
330 Strategic Quality Planning		
331 Development	Establishment of nutrition support program with goals.	
340 Human Resources Management		
341 Planning and Evaluation	• Training and education of admissions personal. • Personnel assigned to nutrition committee, allocated staff, nutrition support teams (with medicine and surgery): development and support.	

TABLE 8.2. ***(continued)***

ACCOUNT / TITLE	ACTIVITY	COST
350 Management of Internal Process Quality		
351 Design and Introduction	• Design, development, deployment of nutrition support program systems and processes for: feeding modes; transition of feeding modes; evaluation of composition and energy requirements; monitors of nutritional status.	
352 Production and Delivery	• Design and development of critical pathway and practice parameters.	
353 Support Services	• HIS/LIS. • Support services: lab, admissions.	
360 Supplier Performance Management		
361 Supplier Quality Management	Identification of necessary equipment, materials, and supplies for program.	
370 Patient Focus: Relationships and Commitment		
371 Patient Satisfaction Determination	• Design and development of outcomes and patient satisfaction surveys.	

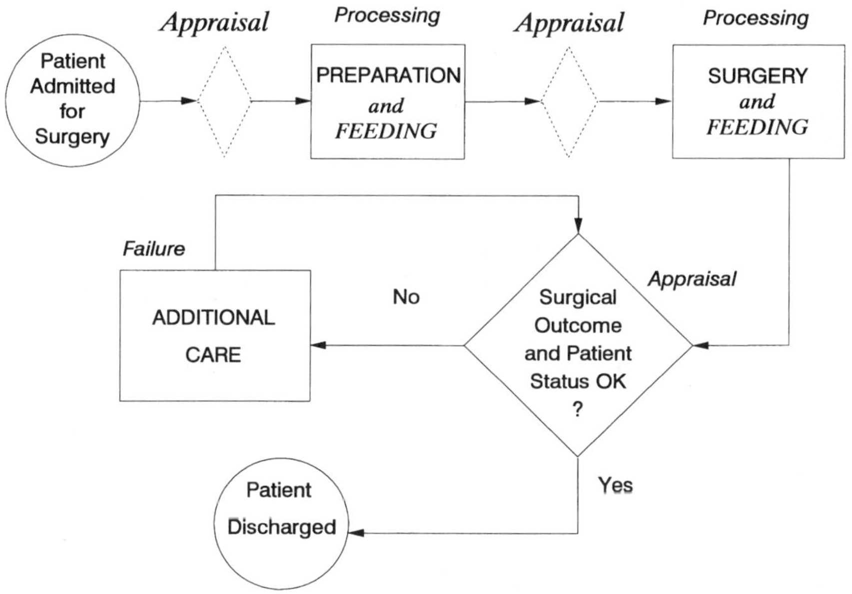

FIGURE 8.9 Flowchart for the Modified Process

The nursing and pharmacy representatives also developed a cost analysis for some subprocess of the elective GI surgery process. They had identified some problems with delivery of medication. They instituted some changes in their subprocess and showed that there were some additional savings by doing a comparison of before (baseline) and after (Table 8.3).

After a six-month period, the team compared the financial results from several patients by those DRGs identified at the beginning. From a decrease in average cycle time for identification of PCM at-risk patients from more than 3 days to just hours, LOS was reduced from 7 to 5 for moderate-risk patients and from 23 to 11 for severe-risk patients, resulting in more than $480,000 in savings and a 17 percent decrease in readmissions.[2]

2. Mears, E. "Prealbumin Nutritional Assessment," study at Leonard J. Chabert Medical Center, Houma, LA, 1994. Also, "Laboratory Utilization for Nutrition Support: Current Practice, Requirements, Expectations," *The Fourteenth Ross Roundtable on Medical Issues.* Savannah, GA: 1993.

TABLE 8.3. **Summary Cost-of-Quality Chart**

PROCESS NAME: *Delivery of medications: cost per service unit (dose)*						
	BASELINE			AFTER MODIFICATION		
Quality Cost Categories	Labor Costs	Other Costs	Total Costs	Labor Costs	Other Costs	Total Costs
Prevention	NA	NA	NA	$0.04	$0.00	$0.04
Processing	$4.98	$7.50	$12.48	$5.13	$7.86	$12.49
Appraisal	NA	NA	NA	$0.03	$0.00	$0.03
Failure	$11.70	$11.25	$22.95	$8.44	$11.78	$20.22

FINE-TUNING COST REDUCTIONS

Reducing cycle time and taking advantage of the opportunities provided by cycle time reduction to improve quality usually reduces costs. Additional steps can further reduce costs without jeopardizing quality and cycle time by focusing on the specific cost-of-quality categories. They are more useful for improvement efforts than traditional expense categories because they reveal what is necessary or useful as shown in Figure 8.10.

Use the following scale to track your cost-reduction progress through customer satisfaction:

- Needs unmet (lowest level of satisfaction).
- Needs met.
- Needs exceeded.
- Needs anticipated (highest level of satisfaction).

The first step is to remove dissatisfiers to advance from not meeting patient needs to meeting them. This requires reducing and eliminating quality and delivery failures by first reducing failure costs. Failure costs are reduced through pre-

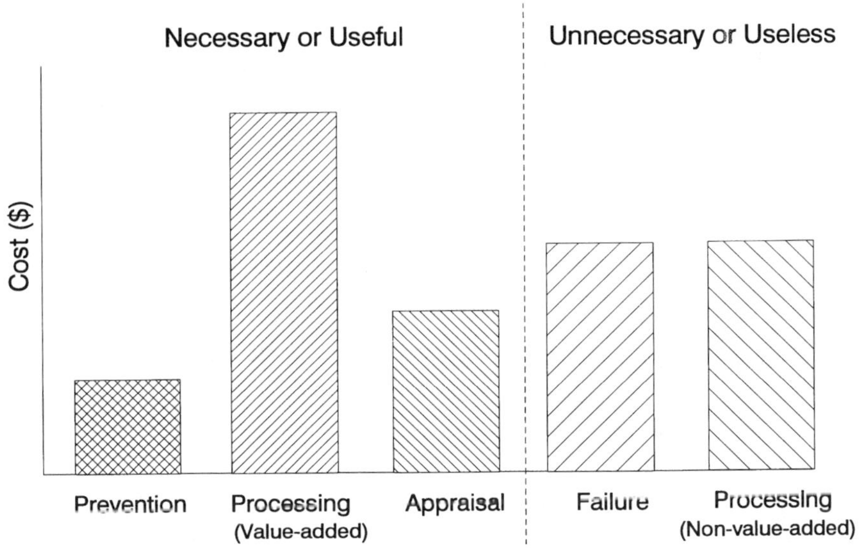

FIGURE 8.10 Cost-of-Quality Categories

vention. This means prevention costs will increase so that failure costs will decrease more than enough to compensate. The second step is to exceed needs by improving on quality and delivery. This means reducing appraisal and processing costs. The third step is to anticipate needs by providing leading-edge services. This means that new services must be brought to market faster with high quality at competitive prices. To do this, you must reduce prevention costs because they are the costs of the quality system.

Reducing costs by improving quality and delivery also requires the use of problem solving, statistics, and learning skills. Information from appraisals and corrective action plus the identification of process activities must flow to the improvement efforts.

Reducing failure costs

To reduce failure costs, five steps are required: gain awareness, create desire, plan, take corrective action, and follow up.[3] Awareness and desire can be created by discovering opportunities. The following questions can help you discover opportunities:

- What percent of your resources are spent on corrective action of failures?
- How do you compare with others with similar processes? Similar patients?
- What is the effect of your failures to the entire organization (consider both directions: patients and suppliers)? Can you estimate a dollar value of this effect?

With desire, you can then plan your strategy to make your patients more satisfied. Consider these questions when deciding strategies and making plans:

- How are failure data used for corrective action and scheduling maintenance?
- How are failure data used to improve products, services, and processes?
- How are failure data used to identify opportunities for improvement, new services, and so on?
- How are failure data used to determine future needs?
- What needs to be improved?
- What information would be helpful to you from accounting and finance? From management? From peers?

Once you have a plan, you must develop corrective actions. Corrective actions address patient dissatisfaction. According to the double-funnel approach to problem solving (see chapter 7), a problem should be stated in terms of the im-

3. Quality Costs Committee. *Guide for Reducing Quality Costs.* Milwaukee, WI: ASQC, 1987, pp. 33.

pact it has on the patient. So, corrective actions require problem solving. Review the double-funnel approach to problem solving and develop your own procedure to include the key journeys: diagnostic and remedial.

Follow-up is required because you will need to improve your failure process. The first attempts may not be effective because there are several issues to consider:

- What are your measures of the quality of your patient feedback process for:
  —Responsiveness to complaints?
  —Frequency of complaints?
  —Frequency of resolution?
- How do you know that your corrective actions have been successful?
- How satisfied are your patients? How do you know?

The types of data necessary for corrective action come from analytic studies. These studies increase your understanding of the process because you understand the particular failure. Review the types of statistical analyses so that you know when to quantify the failure (enumerative statistics) and when you want to understand it (analytic statistics).

Reducing appraisal costs

A patient whose complaint is not heard the first time can cost the hospital several times the cost of immediately addressing his or her needs. A dissatisfied patient may exact revenge by thinking: "You made me wait to get my needs met (delay at admissions), now you can wait for your needs to be met (delay in payment)." Delays in payments and resources spent on pursuing payments reduce profit margins. Patients also have others ways of seeking compensation. They may be late because they know, "I must wait anyway." One consequence of this is addition and extension of lead times. The value of what you deliver decreases.

To help you avoid this type of situation with your patients and to help you reduce appraisal costs, use the questions and keys in Table 8.4 for designing your appraisal system and to identify areas for improvement of appraisal procedures.

A critical aspect of appraisals is the type of information they collect. Effective appraisals are based on well-formed and well-aimed questions. Learning to ask the right questions is the key to improving audits. Questions should focus on system or process weaknesses (e.g., barriers to meeting standards or requirements). For example, it is better to ask *how* things are done, rather than *why* they are not done a certain way. Sometimes asking why directly can sound intimidating. Try asking what the goal or objective of a procedure or activity is rather than, "Why do you do that?"

Reducing processing costs

Three primary ways of reducing processing costs are: value-added analysis, *kaizen*, and reengineering. VA analysis is the simplest to do: identify NVA steps and eliminate them. Typically, this will not alter the quality because it is not intended to do so. It changes efficiency, the rate at which value is added. *Kaizen* is continuous incremental improvements.[4] By finding numerous processing activities that can be improved incrementally over time, you will have made a cumulative significant improvement. Reengineering requires a complete redesign of the process by starting from scratch. Although reengineering requires significantly greater effort to be a benefit, its benefit in return can be magnitudes greater. Typically, reengineering takes advantage of technology to make dramatic gains in productivity, delivery, and efficiency.

---

4. Maasaki, Imai. *Kaizen: The Key to Japan's Competitive Success.* Milwaukee: ASQC Press, 1986.

TABLE 8.4. Keys to Reducing Appraisal Costs

QUESTION	KEY
• Are appraisals done at critical quality decision points only?	Only flowchart the critical steps, not every minute detail. Have quality decision points after the critical activities.
• Are appraisal data used for corrective action, prevention, and maintenance scheduling?	Make sure that appraisal data feed corrective and preventive activities (Q2).
• What is the return on your appraisal costs?	Failure to close the loop and use data for correction and improvement results in high appraisal costs and low prevention costs. Aim to reverse the ratio.
• Does increased sampling increase the reliability of your cost estimates cost-effectively?	As processes become stable and the variation decreases, sampling can be reduced.
• Can automation reduce the total cost (of time, materials, and staffing) and add value?	Before automating or computerizing, determine what failures will be removed and why the automation will remove them. Try another solution before incurring large capital expenses.
• Can lowered-salaried employees do the appraisal?	Delegating has several benefits: empowerment, personnel development, increased trust, and lower costs.
• Can reengineering or restructuring reduce appraisal costs through improved work flow?	Fewer steps reduce the likelihood of errors and are easier to appraise.

TABLE 8.4. (*continued*)

QUESTION	KEY
• Is appraisal performed because of lack of confidence in suppliers?	Shift appraisal of raw materials and supplies to the vendor. Have them show you their statistical process control (SPC) and experimental data to verify their use of quality tools.
• Do different appraisals duplicate work?	The more people are required to sign off on or touch an item, the more likely there will be errors and duplicate appraisals.
• Is the appraisal system based on the assumption of no errors?	Do you consider only negative or only positive results aberrant and unreliable, so you retest until passed? Redesign your tests to improve the false negative rate. Make sure all test results are passed to corrective and preventive activities.
• Is SPC used for evaluation of process capability in addition to process stability?	SPC data not only reveal whether a process is stable, but the data are also useful for more reliably estimating the answer to (Q1) when the process is statistically stable.
• Do audits provide value-added information for improvement?	For example, is there evidence that JCAHO accreditation or CLIA certification as a result of inspection improve patient care?
• Are appraisal costs unnecessarily high or inadequately low?	Laboratories should check their quality control costs versus prevention costs. Hospitals should check the return on utilization review, peer review, and medical audits in improving quality and delivery.

Cycle time management unifies these three ways. Cycle time efficiencies can be improved by focusing on reducing the time to complete the cycle through:

- Removal of interruptions to flow.
- Reduction of the number of steps in the process.

This is VA analysis.

Incremental improvements to quality can be made by reducing the amount of input to the process and simplifying the steps. When fewer things *can* go wrong, fewer things *do* go wrong. By reducing the number of steps and amount of input, you will also reduce the probability and magnitude of variation. Reducing waste and defects in one area typically helps reduce waste and defects in other areas.

Reengineering can occur by recognizing the implicit question posed by cycle time management: If you could reduce cycle time by 50 percent to 99 percent, how would that change this process and related processes and systems? In healthcare, cycle time management can be the basis for reengineering by asking: How can the time to present patient issues, diagnose, provide intervention, begin therapy or treatment, reimburse, be reduced by 50 percent? 90 percent? 99 percent?

Reducing prevention costs

The first step to successful reduction of prevention costs is to accurately assign activities to this cost-of-quality category. The second step is to determine whether the appropriate activities are actually preventing failures and reducing quality costs. Prevention costs are excessive when they do not pay for themselves many times over. Charging the cost of a quality function, department, or work force to prevention costs may be an incorrect accounting of these costs.

Quality control often does not *prevent* failures nor *estimate* quality costs; so it cannot reduce them. Quality control too often functions as an inspection without ever completing the CICS cycle. Quality assurance is also often charged to prevention, but may function merely as an inspection of cross-functional systems.

For a quality function's cost to be appropriately charged to prevention, there must be measurements that show the return on its investment. For example, assigning a team to work on a project for quality improvement seems like a prevention cost. However, if after six months of meetings and planning, the team disbands or is not supported enough to accomplish anything, the cost of the team is no longer a preventive cost: it is most likely an NVA cost.

Evaluating the effect prevention activities have on failures should be a regular part of your job. The following simple experiment can help you assess the effectiveness of your prevention activities:[5]

1. Select a time period during which you processed the same product or service several times.
2. Select the occurrences that represent the three worst cases of processing and product or service quality.
3. Select the occurrences that represent the three best cases of processing and product or service quality.
4. Contrast the characteristics of the process between the best and worst.
5. Contrast the characteristics of the product or service between the best and worst.
6. Use these differences to check whether your prevention activities effectively reduced process failures.

---

5. Bhote, K.R. *World Class Quality: Using Design of Experiments to Make it Happen.* NY: AMACOM, 1991, chapters 7 and 8.

OVERVIEW

Organizations often start with a flurry of teams or projects. Sometime later, senior management wants to know if it was worth the cost and consumption of resources. They should, however, determine ahead of time what would constitute an adequate return on that investment and how it is to be measured. In other words, there must be data confirming the value of continuous improvement.

Tables like 8.1 contain information to substantiate the value of continuous improvement efforts. By having teams and individuals focus on reduction of cycle time, the chances of getting a return on the efforts to make improvements are greatly increased. Two empirical rules-of-thumb from industry are:

1. ¼-2-20 Rule.
2. 3 × 2 Rule.[6]

The first says that for every reduction of cycle time to one-fourth its previous time, results in approximately twice the productivity with a 20 percent reduction in costs. The second says that organizations using cycle time management effectively can achieve up to three times industry average growth rate at twice the profit margins versus organizations that do not use cycle time management.

6. Stalk Jr., George, and Hout, Thomas M. *Competing Against Time.* New York: The Free Press, 1990, pp. 76–79.

9 Implementing Value-Based Cost Management

The senior executive of chapter 1 is finally ready to answer the last two questions:

- How can you financially justify your quality efforts?
- What is your role as senior management?

JUSTIFICATION OF QUALITY EFFORTS

Under value-based cost management, the organization needs to increase employee value, so that employees can increase patient value, so that patients increase business value (recall Figure 8.2). Value is the outcome of process. However, processes are influenced by the physical aspects of the organization and the organizational systems. These are structures. Thirty years ago, Donabedian proposed this structure-process-outcome framework for evaluating the quality of medical care[1] and during the 1980s he refined the framework by identifying its richness and complexity.[2] The practicality

1. Donabedian, A. "Evaluating the quality of medical care," *Milbank Memorial Fund Quarterly: Health and Society* 1966;44:166–206.

2. Donabedian, A. "Models for organizing the delivery of health services and criteria for evaluating them," *Milbank Q* 1972;50:103–54. *The Definition of Quality and Approaches to Its Management,* Vol. 1: *Explorations in Quality Assessment and Monitoring.* Ann Arbor, MI: Health Administration Press, 1980. With Wheeler, JRC and Wyszewianski, L. "Quality, cost, and health: An integrative model," *Med Care* 1982;20:975–92. "The quality of care: How can it be assessed?" *JAMA* 1988;260(12):1743–8.

of this framework depends on establishing relationships between structures and processes on the one hand, and processes and outcomes on the other.[3] However, the appropriate sciences for establishing these relationships—organizational science for the former and behavioral and healthcare sciences for the latter—have not contributed to the desired degree. In addition, this framework does not identify the science needed for establishing the relationship between outcome and structure to close the loop nor the science needed to establish the relationship between structures, processes, outcomes, and costs. Fortunately, value-based cost management identifies the sciences of quality management and finance and accounting as the missing links.

The key to a solution is to find measures of outcomes, processes, and systems that are convertible to costs and that correlate with each other. The actual justification of quality efforts comes from showing that there is a correlation among the business, employee, and patient results (outcomes), your activities (processes), and the structures supporting both (systems). Developing databases showing that the trends in system effectiveness and process performance match the trends in the measures of business, employee, and patient outcomes and satisfaction is therefore critical.

For example, successful efforts to improve your community's cardiovascular health should result in better outcomes for those patients from the community who undergo cardiovascular treatments if everything else were controlled. Because the organization cannot control everything else, you would only expect a positive correlation between indicators of the success of those efforts and the medical outcomes. Increasing trends in measures of effectiveness, efficiency, and adaptability should be matched by appropriate trends in patient satisfaction measures (e.g., patient survey) and your

3. Donabedian, A. "The quality of care: Can it be assessed?" *The Journal of the American Medical Association* 1986;260(12):1743–8.

PVA: PATIENT PERSPECTIVE

- New healthcare services
- Access
- Community partnerships
- Preventive medicine
- Clinical outcomes
- Patient satisfaction

EVA: INTERNAL PERSPECTIVE

- Employee well-being
- Employee development
- Employee retention
- Employee satisfaction
- Patient-focus integration

BVA: LEARNING PERSPECTIVE

- Quality improvement
- Percentage of new services from patients
- Cycle-time efficiency
- Learning cycle-time efficiency
- Time to develop new services

BVA: FINANCIAL PERSPECTIVE

- ABC where feasible
- COQ databases
- Value-added analyses
- Organization cycle-time
- Return on investment
- Cash flow
- Litigation

FIGURE 9.1 Performance Measure Perspectives

clinical outcomes measures (e.g., decreasing trends in mortality and morbidity and increasing trends in functional status).

Developing organizational-level performance measures, as the senior executive of chapter 1 realized, is not an easy task. One of the benefits of value-based cost management is that it simplifies and clarifies the task of identifying performance measures that are critical to your organization's success. Kaplan and Norton suggest a set of performance measures that can address quality, delivery, and cost[4] for all three types of processes. For example, in Figure 9.1, the customer perspective can be used to address patient value-added measures, the internal perspective can be used to address employee value-added measures, and the two remaining per-

4. Kaplan, Robert S., Norton, David P. "The Balanced Scorecard-Measures that Drive Performance." *Harvard Business Review* January/February 1992, pp. 71–9.

spectives, financial and learning, can be used to address business value-added measures.

THE ROLE OF SENIOR MANAGEMENT

Senior management's three basic roles are:

1. To design, develop, deploy, and direct the strategic quality plan.
2. To be owners of the organization's systems.
3. To sponsor quality improvement projects.

These three roles close the loop by connecting the strategic quality plan to the systems supporting the quality improvement efforts. Senior executives also require continuous improvement cycle system (CICS) skills, which they apply to the organization's systems.

Strategic quality plan

The senior executive leaders, sometimes collectively called the quality council, consist of the highest-ranking official and his or her direct reports (e.g., the chief executive officer and the chief medical, nursing, and financial officers). This group's first role is to develop a strategic quality plan based on information about the organization's current and past performance and what they believe the future competitive situation will be. The plan includes long- and short-term strategies and goals. To achieve these goals using the selected strategies requires a commitment of resources that define the budget and provide definitions for patient, employee, and business measures and indicators. As the fiscal year progresses, analyses will be required on both financial and nonfinancial measures.

The patient impact is defined not only by clinical outcomes and patient satisfaction but also by the organization's relationships with its vendors or suppliers. Poor relationships with them can result in not only poor quality materials and supplies, but delays in their delivery, which affect total costs, employee morale, and the quality of healthcare services patients receive. The employee impact is defined by development, retention, and value-added rates. The business impact is defined by the organization's financial success and its relationship with its employees. These fiscal strategies define patient-value, employee-value, and business-value activities.

In the short-term, the goals will be achieved by strategies that have an impact on the patient and community, the employees, and the business. This requires that senior management develop a list of healthcare issues to address by their strategic and marketing plans. These can be grouped into community healthcare issues and patient healthcare issues (see Table 9.1). For example, the senior management team may choose to focus on preventable malnutrition of hospitalized patients as one of their quality issues.

From this list, the senior management team develops goals that should stretch the capacity of the organization. For example, they may include:

- Reduce heart attacks by 50 percent.
- Reduce extended lengths of stay by 30 percent.
- Increase childhood immunizations by 40 percent.
- Add two new services within the next 12 months.

Other possibilities may be to focus exclusively on waste and non-value-added activities at the strategic level:

- Reduce the cost of poor quality by 35 percent in 18 months.
- Improve cycle-time efficiency three-fold in 18 months.

For example, the organization may select a goal of reducing by 50 percent the number of cases of protein-calorie malnutrition (PCM).

TABLE 9.1. Critical Healthcare Issues

COMMUNITY	PATIENT
• Access • Cardiovascular health • Childhood immunization • Integrated services with other community services (e.g., for battered women or abused children) • Racial/economic health status inequalities • Sudden infant death syndrome • AIDS/HIV • Worksite risks • Teenage health issues (e.g., pregnancy, drug abuse, alcoholism)	• Wait, delay, storage, transport times • Caesarean sections • Malnutrition • Inappropriate practices • Patient education programs • OR turnover • Resource use by service or physician. • Discharged patients with abnormal results • Billing errors

Keeping track of the progress toward these goals through the correlations of process measures with clinical outcome and patient satisfaction measures is senior management's responsibility.

ORGANIZATIONAL SYSTEM OWNERS

All quality efforts focus primarily on process improvements (see chapter 3). However, processes are constrained by the structure in which they operate. That environment is in turn created by the organization's systems. Ineffective, inefficient, and inflexible systems are the primary source of most of an organization's waste and nonconformances. The responsibility for managing these systems belongs to the senior executive team.

So, the senior executive leaders' second responsibility is to be process owners of the organization's systems. This means that they are responsible for the design, development, deployment, and direction of the organization's systems. This responsibility includes:

- Improving the systems under which the to-be-improved processes operate to maintain the gains.
- Reallocating regained resources to value-added activities.

Organizational systems

Most organizations can identify eight areas that need to be addressed by senior management through development of systems:

1. Leadership.
2. Strategic planning.
3. Information and analysis.
4. Human resources.
5. Products and services (e.g., medical/clinical).
6. Support functions.
7. Suppliers.
8. Customers (e.g., patient, community, other stakeholders).[5]

---

5. National Institute of Standards and Technology. *The Malcolm Baldrige National Quality Award.* Gaithersburg, MD: U.S. Department of Commerce Technology Administration.

In healthcare, another system can be added:

9. Accreditation and assessment.[6]

Organizational systems also require measures. While the medical field has been developing measures for clinical processes and outcomes, they have relied on the Joint Commission on Accreditation of Healthcare Organizations and the National Committee for Quality Assessment for system measures. However, these standards, criteria, and measures provide a basic level of assessment that severely limits their use as continuous improvement measures.[7]

More appropriate measures have been developed for the Baldrige 1995 Health Care Pilot Program. These criteria focus on the systems, their level of deployment, and their effectiveness in achieving their purpose as defined by the organization.

The value-based cost management approach implies that quality management systems consist of five elements:

1. Goal. The goal can be stated using the same parameters that a problem statement has: *Where* will *who* do *how much* of *what* by *when?*
2. Management procedures, including:
   —Communication and interactions.
   —Allocation of resources.
   —Removal of barriers.
   —Recognition and reward.
3. Operating procedures, including:
   —Processing (service or production).
   —Support services.

---

6. National Institute of Standards and Technology. *The Malcolm Baldrige National Quality Award: 1995 Health Care Pilot Program.* Gaithersburg, MD: U.S. Department of Commerce Technology Administration.

7. Jackson, F. "The Baldrige/JCAHO Crosswalk," *Quality Connection* 1994;3(4):4–7.

—Information.
—Documentation.

4. Measures, including:
—Quality.
—Delivery.
—Cost.
—Sales.
—Profitability.

5. Continuous improvement procedures, including:
—Corrective action.
—Preventive action.
—Appraisal.
—Problem solving.

For senior executive leaders who wish to incorporate a value-based cost management system, the National Association of Accountants (NAA) makes five recommendations regarding making changes to systems and introducing an organizationwide cost management system:

1. Have realistic expectations.
2. Demonstrate how quality increases and cost reductions will occur.
3. Estimate the time for the organization to see the benefits.
4. Describe in the common language of dollars.
5. Monitor and measure the progress and results.[8]

The NAA also recommends an 11-step procedure for implementing a cost of quality system. These steps can be sim-

8. Atkinson, J.H., Hohmer, G., Mundt, B., Troxel, R.B., and Whichell, W. *Current Trends in Cost of Quality: Linking the Cost of Quality to Continuous Improvement.* Montvale, NJ: National Association of Accountants, 1991.

plified to six steps and applied to the implementation of the cost-of-quality categories, activity-based cost accounting and value-added analysis. Table 9.2 shows the six steps for designing, developing and evaluating the three parts of an organizationwide value-based cost management approach.

Reallocation of resources

Once non-value added costs have been reduced, resources allocated to those activities are freed. Unless these are reallocated to value-added activities, they may still be thought of as expenses without increasing value. The same is true with the activities originally allocated to address poor quality. One option for these resources is for them to be allocated to prevention activities, either for redesigning existing systems and processes or creating new systems and processes for existing or new products and services. Another option is to allocate these resources to increase productivity, as illustrated in Figure 5.12. For example, reengineering a process usually results in improved productivity with fewer people. Planning for this change would include retraining employees so the organization can shift them from their current jobs to other jobs rather than laying them off.

SPONSOR QUALITY IMPROVEMENT PROJECTS

Quality improvement projects can contribute most to an organization's strategic plan if they are coordinated and focused on one or two goals and strategies. One approach to doing this is to assign multifunctional teams to support the organization's goals (see Figure 9.2) through quality-improvement projects that require the use of their CICS skills. The role of the senior management team is to select, direct, and support these teams—that is:

- To identify the team members and assign them to appropriate projects.

TABLE 9.2. Steps for Implementing Value-Based Cost Management

Step number	ABC	VA Analysis	COQ
1. Establish operational definitions	Cost objects	Value-added activities	Cost of quality objects
2. Identify elements	Costs associated with cost objects	Activities associated with cost objects	Costs and COQ categories
3. A. Identify information sources or B. Develop a system	A. Cost information B. For assigning costs to to cost objects	A. Activity information B. For assigning activities to value-added categories	A. Cost information B. For assigning costs to cost-of-quality categories
4. Design forms	Reports and graphs	Reports and graphs	Reports and graphs
5. Design procedures	Data collection	Data collection	Data collection
6. Establish baselines	On profitability of service or product lines	On value-added versus non-value-added: costs and efficiencies	On cost of quality categories: distribution
7. Design continuous improvement plans	Review, revise, repeat	Review, revise, repeat	Review, revise, repeat

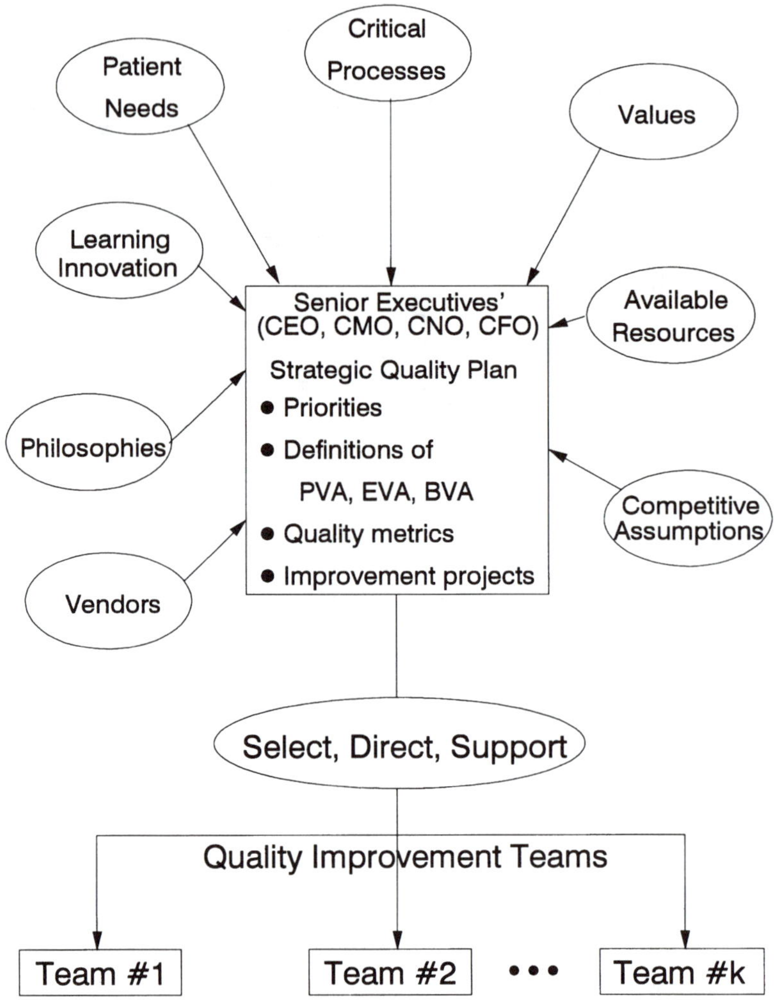

FIGURE 9.2 Multifunctional Teams

- To provide them with the strategic quality plan and the goal to which the team is to contribute, define the team's mission and duration, and evaluate its progress.
- To remove barriers to their success (e.g., to provide them with education, training, facilities, resources, time, encouragement, and recognition).

Senior management's efforts to improve systems are also supported by individuals who have specific missions and goals defined for them. Departments or units and individuals are informed about the strategic quality plan as it cascades through the organization (see Figure 2.3). Individuals in turn work to improve their own processes using the skills defined by the CICS.

Each team is then responsible for identifying specific process measures that define effectiveness, efficiency, and adaptability. When improvements are made in these process areas, there should be a corresponding improvement in the outcome measures. One way to keep track of the teams's progress on their projects is to use a chart such as the one in Table 9.3. This type of chart and report encourages the use of quantitative measures while focusing on value and expectations.

For example, the malnutrition team could have been just one of several teams to address an organizationwide effort to improve all surgical processes. After the senior management team disseminates the strategy and goals to all employees, it could ask for volunteers for six teams:

1. Patient-focus team.
2. Clinical team.
3. Human resource team.
4. Support service team.
5. Information and analysis team.
6. Supplier quality team.

Volunteers for each team are responsible for developing substrategies and actions for achieving the goal. The malnutrition team of chapter 8 is one variation of a clinical team.

Each team is given different missions and projects. For example, there are several issues raised from an organizational perspective, some of which affect PCM directly:

TABLE 9.3. Project Recordkeeping

Goals Strategies								
		OUTCOMES			VALUE			
PROJECTS	TEAMS	EXPECTED	ACTUAL	COSTS	PATIENT	EMPLOYEE	BUSINESS	

- How long does it take to register hospitalized patients?
- How long does it take for a patient registered to be physically in his or her assigned bed?
- How long does it take to assess a patient's severity or acuity level?
- How accessible are medical and financial records to the teams?
- How will cross-functional issues be resolved?
- Will administration support increases in expenditures in one department if the total costs are reduced and total quality is improved?
- How long does it take for patients at risk for PCM to be so identified and classified?
- Are estimates of direct nursing costs and pharmacy costs accurate enough for assessing profitability?
- How satisfied are employees with their work, well-being, and ability to contribute?
- Are the system constraints causing low employee morale, which in turn causes low patient satisfaction?
- How long does it take for these patients to be billed?
- How long does it take for payments to be received?
- How satisfied are these patients with: registration, the room, meals, attendance by staff, and so on?
- How satisfied are employees with the quality and relationships with the organization's vendors?

Each of these issues could be prioritized and assigned to different teams so that each team is working toward the same goal. Conflicts for team resources could be resolved in favor of teams showing a greater potential for a return in improved quality and delivery and decreased costs. Each team would also generate its own measures of effectiveness, efficiency, and adaptability. To establish cost baselines, the question of whether ABC would provide better cost estimates than current ones could always be raised.

Summary

We have come full circle. Looking back at Figure 2.5, we started with the thoughts of senior management as it prepared its organization for the quickly changing environment of healthcare. These thoughts were translated into specific questions that addressed how the organization as a whole and its individual components could function more effectively through the use of a total quality management philosophy. This required integrating different aspects of the organization: its suppliers, employees, and customers; its structures, processes, and expected outcomes; long-range planning, short-term goals, and day-to-day

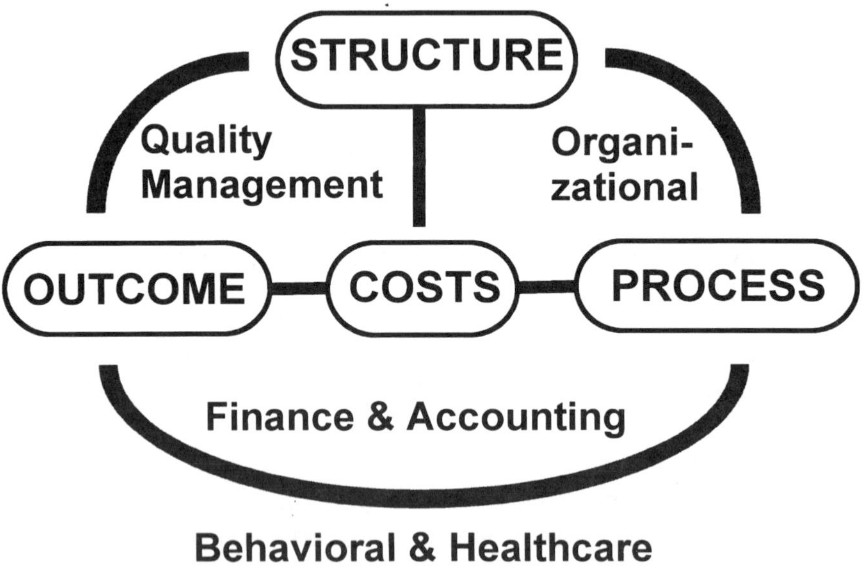

FIGURE 9.3 The Structure-Process-Outcome Model

activities; measures for systems, processes, and outcomes; time, quality, costs, and delivery; and skills.

By expanding Donabedian's structure-process-outcome model as shown in Figure 9.3, we identified the sciences and a set of measures that can be used to establish relationships among all these factors. This further enriches an already complex framework for assessing quality in healthcare. The model enables us to develop a comprehensive approach called value-based cost management that defines the different measures needed, identifies the skills required and how to use them, links new financial and accounting tools with measures of quality, time, and delivery, and provides the methods for implementation.

With value-based cost management, we have answered all the questions raised by our executive. We now wait for a new set of questions, so even this approach can be continuously improved.

List of Key Terms

Activity-based costing A method of assigning costs as activities consume them. By recognizing the causal relationships between cost drivers, activities, and resources, the accuracy of cost estimates is improved. By tracking costs in reverse order of the demand flow, activity-based costing can estimate costs in real time and at the individual patient level.

Analytic statistics Statistical analysis useful for continuous improvement because it identifies the sources or causes of noncomformances. Analytic statistics are used to answer item Q2 in the Continuous Improvement Cycle System.

Balanced Scorecard A set of organization-level measures of value that balance the needs of the business, employees, and patients. With these measures, senior management is in a better position to lead, manage, and adjust the organization than traditional measures that are unbalanced toward just the business needs.

Continuous Improvement Cycle System A framework that identifies the necessary activities and skills for continuous improvement. The cycle consists of repeatedly answering two questions:

Q1. What are the current quality, delivery, and cost levels?

Q2. How can these levels be improved?

The five skills needed to answer these questions are:

1. The ability to analyze quality and delivery as costs.
2. The ability to understand process variation.
3. The ability to learn and acquire new knowledge.

4. The ability to solve problems based on that new knowledge.
5. The ability to manage cycle time.

Cost of quality A method for reducing costs *by* improving quality by recognizing the relationship between resource consumption and quality as defect-free services and products. Four new expense categories relate processes and costs; prevention costs are incurred when processes are designed or redesigned, processing costs are incurred when processes are used, appraisal costs are incurred when processes are evaluated, and failure costs are incurred when process outputs are corrected.

Cycle time management A method for resolving the organizational time-quality-cost dilemma by defining time as *cycle time* and quality as *defect free.* Cycle time management argues that reducing cycle time supports cost reduction and quality improvement in three ways: 1. by increasing the amount of information and knowledge about a process; 2. by increasing the number of opportunities to use that information and knowledge to improve the process; and 3. decreasing the labor cost per unit of output. Improving quality also reduces costs by reducing failure costs.

Enumerative statistics Statistical analysis useful for continuous improvement because it provides estimates of how much nonconformance there is. Enumerative statistics are used to answer item Q1 in the Continuous Improvement Cycle System.

Quality organizational system An organizational system comprising five elements: 1. goals, 2. management procedures that address communication, interactions, allocation of resources, removal of barriers, recognition and reward; 3. operating procedures; 4. measures that address business-, employee-, and patient-value-added processes; and 5. continuous improvement procedures that include corrective and preventive actions, appraisal, and problem solving.

Process A process is a repeated sequence of activities that consume resources by transforming one thing to another to satisfy customer needs. There are three types of processes: business-value-added, employee-value-added, and patient-value-added. Business-value-added processes are those processes whose customers (e.g., the organization itself, suppliers, distributors, partners and allies, shareholders) seek financial value. Employee-value-added processes are those processes whose customers seek employment value (e.g., wages, benefits, career development, education, training, sense of self-worth.) Patient-value-added processes are those processes whose customers seek health-related value (e.g., patients and communities seeking clinical and personal services for their physiological and psychological well-being.)

Value-added analysis A method of identifying acitivies and their assigned resources that do not add value to the intended customer. Value-added analysis recognizes three types of processes: business-value-added, employee-value-added, and patient-value-added processes.

Value-based cost management A cost management framework for linking structures, processes, outcomes, quality, and costs by identifying the measures of organizational systems, work environment, and financial relations needed to establish the relationships. When applied to healthcare, value-based cost management identifies the types of measures needed to link practice parameters, critical pathways, clinical outcomes (patient value), business value, employee value, quality, and costs.

Index